Re-centring Mother Earth:
Ecological Reading of Contemporary Works of Fiction

Andrew Nyongesa

Tendai Rinos Mwanaka

Mwanaka Media and Publishing Pvt Ltd,
Chitungwiza Zimbabwe
*
Creativity, Wisdom and Beauty

Publisher: *Mmap*
Mwanaka Media and Publishing Pvt Ltd
24 Svosve Road, Zengeza 1
Chitungwiza Zimbabwe
mwanaka@yahoo.com
mwanaka13@gmail.com
https://www.mmapublishing.org
www.africanbookscollective.com/publishers/mwanaka-media-and-publishing
https://facebook.com/MwanakaMediaAndPublishing/

Distributed in and outside N. America by African Books Collective
orders@africanbookscollective.com
www.africanbookscollective.com

ISBN: 978-1-77921-331-0
EAN: 9781779213310

© Andrew Nyongesa 2022

All rights reserved.
No part of this book may be reproduced or transmitted in any form or by any means, mechanical or electronic, including photocopying and recording, or be stored in any information storage or retrieval system, without written permission from the publisher

DISCLAIMER
All views expressed in this publication are those of the author and do not necessarily reflect the views of *Mmap*.

Table of Contents

Chapter One: Introduction..1
1.1   Purpose, Scope and Context of the Study.............................1
1.2   Literature Review...9
1.3   The Statement of the Problem...14
Chapter Two: Mother Nature and Social Spectrum: Class and Traditions in Contemporary Novels...17
Mother Nature and Social Condition: Violence and Migrancy in Nadifa Mohamed's *Black Mamba Boy* and Nyongesa's "The Sordid Boon"...18
Patriarchy and Infibulation: Mother Nature's Autocracy in Contemporary Novels..30
Mother Nature, Human Behaviour and Livelihoods: Economic Practices in John Steinbeck's *The Pearl* and Mativo's "On the Market Day".......41
Chapter Three: Mother Nature and Politics: Ecological Attributes and Governance...56
3.1 Slavery and Colonialism: Ecological Setting and Growth of Despotism..58
3.2 Slavery and Development of Autocracy: Violation of Human Rights in Slave Narratives and Novels..61
3.3 Colonialism and Rise of Dictatorship: Violation of Human Rights in Contemporary Novels..70
3.4 The Industrial Revolution and Autocratic Parenting: Mother Nature and Facts in Dicken's *Hard Times*..83
3.5. Mother Nature and the Council of Elders: Consensus and Democracy in Contemporary Novels......................................95
3.6. Hot Deserts and Dictatorial Regimes: Military Regimes in Contemporary Works of fiction...103
Chapter Four: Mother Nature and Religion: Ecological Environment and Belief Systems in Contemporary Novels..................................117

4.1 Mother Nature and the Patriarch: The Sea and the First Man in Ihimera's *The Whale Rider*..................119
4.2 Mother Nature and Somali Indigenous Religion: *Wagar* and the Crow in Contemporary Somali Fiction..................128
4.3 The Eminence of Mother Nature: Mountain and *Mugumo* Altars in Contemporary Fiction..................136
CHAPTER FIVE: Ecology and Pathology: Mother Nature and Mental Illness in Contemporary Postcolonial Literatures..................145
5.1 Hot, Dry Weather and Mental Illness: The Fragmented Self and Disorders of the Self..................147
5.2 Cold Weather and Mental ill-health: The Fragmented Self in *Rhy's Voyage in the Dark*..................160
Chapter 6: CHAPTER SUMMARIES, CONCLUSIONS AND RECOMMENDATIONS FOR FUTURE STUDIES..................171
Recommendations for Future Tasks..................174
Mmap Nonfiction and Academic books..................177

Chapter One: Introduction

1.1 Purpose, Scope and Context of the Study

The modern society has elevated homocentric perspectives that degrade and neglect the ecological surroundings in which humankind lives. The high and low cultural aspects of modernism tends to focus on the material wellbeing and places humanity at the centre of the universe. This tenet of modernism no doubt alienates humanity from the natural environment. According to Devall and Sessions (1985) in their exegesis of modernity observe:

> Contemporary humanistic ethical theory is ineradicably anthropocentric, designed specifically to deal with the problems of human interaction. When the attempt is made to extend this theory to other animals [...] they are accorded much less moral consideration than humans. (55)

In their perspective, Devall and Sessions demonstrate the homocentric nature of modernism as it elevates humankind above Mother Nature. Ascribed to higher rank, humankind is highly cherished and therefore given authority to manipulate and use natural resources as they wish. For instance, it does not bother anyone if a human person slaughters all his livestock to entertain friends and relatives. First, the individual is doing it for his good, and better still for the good of society. Not one person will think about the animals as it is believed they exist for the sake of humankind. In fact no one remembers the animals' impact on the ecosystem before they were slaughtered. Kamanzi A. (2011) refers to this homocentric aspect of modernity as Egocetrism defined as a type of ethos that "allows individuals to extract and use natural resources to enhance their own lives" (211). Kamanzi expounds that the Egocentric ethos is the underlying impulse that motivates modern individuals to believe they are responsible for their own salvation through good action (211). Therefore, if a person believes they should slaughter all their animals to save themselves from seclusion and hunger, then all their contemporaries will just congratulate and join them for a celebration.

Better still, anything done for the good of fellow human beings is elevated above what is done for the good of Mother Nature. Obsessed with homocentric attributes, the modern society will reserve prestigious awards for persons that contribute towards to the betterment of humanity than those who contribute towards the ecological environment. According to Mill (1957), something good is related to the general interests of society, the interests of the whole and the good of the whole" (22-23). As long as what the individual is preoccupied with does not harm other members of the society then they should be left to pursue their ambitions. Kamanzi refers to this homocentric aspect as nos-centric ethos. Individuals are appraised for doing things that benefit a greater number of people without any consideration for the impact of the action on the ecological environment.

In the previous anecdote of slaughtering animals, Mill will appraise the act because many people will enjoy the feast and retire home happy. Secondly, the poor and hungry will have the meal for the day since animals were *meant* for human use. Christian attendants will cite scripture, (Genesis 1.26-30) to show how the creator of the universe gave humankind authority to use plants and animals for food. If there are any trees in the home that cooks will need to light fires to roast meet, the trees will be cut down for that purpose. Whereas traditional beliefs in Africa and beyond underscored the sanctity of nature, the modernist ethos transgresses this because it borrows the aforementioned homocentric attributes of Christianity and Judaism. Philosophers who established enlightenment, which is at the crux of modernism demonstrated support for this homocentric ethos to a certain extent. Bacon (1620) for instance wrote:

> Those who have handled sciences have been either men of experiment or men of dogmas. The men of experiment are like the ant, they only collect and use; the reasoners resemble spiders, who make cobwebs out of their own substance. But the bee takes a middle course: it gathers its material from the flowers of the garden and of the field, but transforms and digests it by a power of its own. (XCV)

Bacon in this aphorism views science as one of the homocentric field of knowledge because the men of science can only use Mother Nature to achieve their ends. Like the ant, the physical scientist has the authority to collect and use elements of the ecosystem without her retaliation. Just like spiders, the scientists will use the materials gathered from Mother Nature to manufacture new products for human use and finally, there are bees that pick nectar from Mother Nature to manufacture beautiful products for human consumption. As a father of Science, Bacon places the ecosystem at the mercy of humankind which accounts for the negligence and irresponsible exploitation of the ecosystem in the contemporary society.

Modernist scholars continued to expound on Bacon's utilitarianism that relegates Mother Nature to the very periphery of life on Mother Earth. Spedding et al. (1870) for instance writes:

> The new man of science must not think that the inquisition of nature is in any part interdicted or forbidden. Nature must be bound into service and made a slave, put in constraint, and moulded by the mechanical arts. The searchers and spies of nature were to discover her plots and secrets. ... Only by digging further and further in the mine of natural knowledge, could mankind discover that lost dominion (of nature). (20)

It is interesting how humankind that is brought on to Mother Earth and starts life with full dependence on her water, oxygen, plant and animal products starts bragging as Spending et. al do. How is it possible that a two year toddler can brag to compel the sun to "be bound into service and made a slave?" what does the toddler know about the chemical processes that enable the sun to produce light for the planet? Suppose the toddler were Spedding and his colleagues, it is still impossible for them to explain what prevents the sun from moving towards the planets and unleashing insurmountable desertification. If indeed Mother Nature is a slave to humanity, why have we not eradicated hot and cold deserts on Earth? Sahara desert has been in existence for millions of years. Why have we not nipped earthquakes in the bud? Why is humankind unable to stop cyclones, tsunamis and typhoons that claim thousands of lives across the globe? One is left to wonder where these powerful scientists had gone when a severe earthquake struck Nepal in 2015, killed 9,000 people and reduced 600,000 structures to rabble. The sophisticated American planes only arrived in Kathmandu to evacuate survivors to hospitals and safer towns of Nepal. Is this how humankind lords it over Mother Nature?

African scholars have associated this homocentric ethos of modernism with Western tradition. In his eco-critical reading of African Literature, Okuyade (2013) observes that in Africa, "nature is not the Other as in the industrialized and urbanized West…but is an integral part of his world order" (viii). Citing Achebe's *Things Fall Apart*, Okuyade underscores the sanctity with which African societies revered Mother Nature through their cultural heritage. Kimanzi reiterates Okuyade's assertion that the modernist ethos has always otherized Mother Nature. He writes, "[w]hile before Bacon, the relationship between human beings and nature was characterised by an "I-thou" ethic, which was in many times dominated by propitiation before any act of using the "thou", Bacon's transformation resulted into an "I-Other" ethic" (208). Whereas before the scientific revolution humankind saw themselves as part of Mother Nature, they crowned themselves as superior to Nature after the revolution. According Staszak (2008), othering refers to stigmatization of difference (9). Because Mother Nature is not as we are, the difference is exaggerated and stigmatized.

As much Kimanzi claims that Bacon was majorly responsible for othering of Mother Nature, this book takes the view that his philosophical works were misinterpreted. There is a sense in which Bacon also expressed the essential role of Mother Nature, which his successors shoved aside to perpetuate their homocentric ethos. In the first aphorism of his *New organ*, he writes:

> Man, being the servant and interpreter of Nature, can do and understand so much and so much only as he has observed in fact or in thought of the course of nature. Beyond this he neither knows anything nor can do anything. (I)

In this aphorism, we do not find othering of Mother Nature; on the contrary, Bacon elevates Nature because all scientific knowledge can only be accessed through observation of Nature. Humankind is the servant: Nature is the master because without Nature, the scientist will have nothing to observe. This study therefore disagrees with Kimanzi and other scholars that associate homocentric ethos with Bacon's ideas. In the third aphorism, Bacon asserts, "[h]uman knowledge and human power meet in one; for where the cause is not known, the effect cannot be produced. Nature to be commanded must be obeyed." As much as humanity may possess some power over Nature, they have to obey it. Bacon demonstrates the relationship between humankind and nature is two way; she controls us and we control it because we have to obey before we order her.

It is also confounding for a person who comes to observe and learn something from me changes overnight and starts bragging that they are the *self* and I am the *other*. This is preposterous because I already knew myself before he came to observe me. For example, before humankind studied how lightning is formed, lightning already existed. How can this scientist now claim to be more superior to lightning? Is it because he makes a lightning arrestor? Has the arrestor stopped lighting from forming? Before solar panels were made, the sun existed; shining for billions of humankind. Is it not ridiculous for the inventor of the Solar panel to claim that they are superior to the sun? In the same way, Michael Faraday, having invented electricity, cannot brag of being superior to the sun. Whereas Faraday has to struggle to move conductors in a magnetic flux, the sun just rises and produces light to dozens of planets for seasons and years.

As the title, *Re-centring Mother Earth: Ecological Reading of Contemporary Works of Fiction* suggests, this book seeks to restore the principal influence of Mother Nature in human life. Individual literary critics have demonstrated how literary writers have deliberately presented the impact of Mother Nature on the lives of characters. However, most of them have hardly demonstrated the indispensable role of ecological environment on the political, social and religious attributes of human life. Although most scholars single out human greed and imperialism as the prime causes of historical events such as colonialism, war, slavery and industrialisation, this book extends it by investigating the influence of Mother Nature in the political, cultural, religious aspects of human life in contemporary novels.

This book is close textual analysis of works of fiction from any regions of the globe. The wide scope of choice of texts is deliberate because ecological issues are global and should be given the gravity they deserve in every continent. This study would have used academic and journalistic primary texts, but I choose literary texts because literature has the capacity to speak to hearts rather than minds of audiences. According to Brueggemann (1989):

> To address the issue of a truth greatly reduced requires us to be *poets that speak against a prose world*. The terms of that phrase are readily misunderstood. By prose I refer to a world that is organised in settled formulae, so that even pastoral prayers and love letters sound like memos (48)

Brueggemann in the line "speak against prose world" suggests that works of art possess certain unconventionality that will invert the homocentric ethos that has constantly relegated Mother Nature. The phrases "organised in settled formulae" is a snide reference to enlightenment tenets that have influenced most fields of knowledge to bolster othering of Mother Nature. Indeed even most literary writers have also adopted a homocentric approach to issues. Nature is only appealed to for aesthetic purposes or out of desire to express homocentric subjects. Lawrence Buell (2005) therefore establishes a criteria of what is considered an ecological literary work: "[t]he nonhuman environment is present not merely as a framing device, the human interest is not … the only legitimate interest, human accountability to the environment is part of the text's ethical orientation and finally there is some sense of the environment as a process" (9). Bull suggests that although some literary writers use images from Mother Nature, they only serve an aesthetic purpose to express homocentric ethos. Such literary works may not be selected for analysis in this study. The study will be more interested in works of fiction that also address ecological concerns besides human interests. Works of fiction with natural catastrophes such as droughts, cyclones, typhoons and tsunamis adhere Buell's assertion of "environment as a process" (9), in other words, the drought must have arisen from prolonged instances of deforestation.

This study will deviate from Buell's criteria of ecological works of fiction in instances where the literary author suggests the centrality of Mother Nature without direct mention of ecological involvement. Indeed ecological readings have been done on many writers of creative fiction, but this study fills a gap as described in the next section.

1.2 Literature Review

The purpose of this subsection is to analyse similar studies to avoid replication of studies and locate a gap for this study. As much as ecological concerns in relation to literature have been done, most of them do not give Mother Nature her pertinent role in the political, social and religious aspects of humanity. This section begins with general studies in ecology and then turns focus to literary studies.

There are scholars that have emphasized the role of the ecological environment in human life. Russell et al. (2013) observes that nature or ecosystem contributes to human well-being as it affects the physical, mental, spiritual health, inspiration and identity of individuals (p. 473). Indeed Russell et. al recognize the impact of the ecosystem and hence denounce homocentric ethos discussed above. However, they fail to recognize the role of literature in expressing serious environmental concerns. Whereas Russell's focus is on general ecological studies, this book is an eco-critical reading of contemporary novels to show how Mother Nature permeates the political, social and religious aspects of life.

Secondly, psychologists have underscored the nexus between othering and mental illness. Fanon (1961, 250) avers that othering results in psychic collapse of their victims. Singling out colonialism as political othering, Fanon points it out as the major cause of mental illness. Fanon's study contributes to this study by expounding on the concept of "othering" with regard to Nature. As Kamanzi and Okuyade observe, modernity has the tendency to otherize Nature, because of its inherence difference. While to Fanon, mental illness arises from othering by fellow humans, this study investigates ecological causes of mental illness in contemporary fiction.

Literary writers and artists have demonstrated how scientific and industrial revolutions affected the natural environment and humankind. Isabella Ballarin (2019) observes that the industrial revolution alienated society from the ecological environment in Charles Dickens' *Hard Times*. She demonstrates how the fact filled culture of the industrial revolution drew children away from their ecological environment (6). The homocentric ethos is evident in the way the child is affected by the revolution. While Ballarin's focuses on how the industrial revolution affected Mother Nature in Dicken's *Hard Times*, this study investigates how Mother Nature influenced industrial revolution in many other works of contemporary fiction.

Literary critics have published eco-critical studies of Gracia Marquez works, particularly the role of nature in the themes in *One Hundred Years of Solitude*. Raymond Williams points out that the hyperbolic rains in Marquez's *One Hundred Years of Solitude* reiterate the purifying attribute of the Biblical flood. He adds that weather changes in the novel are sometimes a source of humour. Indeed Nature in this study just appears as an aesthetic element that according to Buell (2005) disqualifies some aspects of the work from eco-criticism. While William's focus is ecological aspects of Marquez single work, this book will examine the effect of the ecological environment on the social, political, economic and religious aspects of characters in dozens of novels across the globe.

Moreover, literary critics in Africa have demonstrated how novelists have focused on the nexus between literature and Mother Nature. Lusinga (2016) observes that Ole Kulet's works celebrate the rich biodiversity of Maasai's natural environment. Lusinga avers that Kulet has a knack for knitting powerful images of the community's flora and fauna in his fiction" (p. 3). Whereas Lusinga's focus is on ecological representations in Kulet's *Vanishing Herds* and *The Hunter,* the focus of this book is on the impact of the ecological environment on the political, religious, social, economic life of characters in contemporary novels in Africa and beyond. Furthermore, this study will select any novel or short story that suggests the impact of Mother Nature on characters without deliberate description of environmental degradation.

Literary critics have also demonstrated how the ecological environment determines the choice of the cultural practices of people for instance patriarchy and female genital mutilation. Nyongesa A. (2021) shows how the ecological environment compels the Maasai community to adopt patriarchal cultural practice in Kulet's *Blossoms of the Savannah*. While Nyongesa's article underscores the influence of Mother Nature on cultural choices in one African novel, this study extends Mother Nature's influence to political, social and religious choices in contemporary novels across the globe.

Scholars have raised eco-critical concerns in selected works of African Literature. Ogaga Okuyade (2013) examines how African literary writers show their ecological concerns from West, East and Southern Africa. Okuyade observes that in Africa, "Nature is not the Other as in the industrialized and urbanized West…but is an integral part of his world order" (viii). While Okuyade's study is relevant to this study because both are eco-critical readings, the two differ because this study focuses on the supremacy of Mother Nature on every aspect of human life. Whereas Okuyade's focus is African Literature, this study widens the scope to global works of fiction to give ecological concerns the gravity they deserve.

Scholars have demonstrated the nexus between Mother Nature and religious aspects of humankind. Mercy Oduyoye (2020) observes that to the Akan, "[t]he whole Earth is sacred, and any place can be a place for worship. Mother Earth, therefore, is a sacred space" (xiii). Oduyoye's assertion underscores the impact of the ecological environment on religion of a people. While Oduyoye's focus is theological study of African communities, this study extends the impact of Mother Nature on a broad spectrum of human life through characters of contemporary novels in our world today.

In their criticism, Ghudhlanga, Muganiwe and Gube (2022) demonstrate how literary authors bring out the environmental crisis, the focus on Africa and people of African descent; the utilisation of the creative as opposed to the usual non-fiction approach, the role of religion in the search for solutions to the environmental crisis as well as the usage of gender as an analytical category (16). Using literary works and fork tales from many parts of Africa, the contributors analyse the aforementioned themes with bent towards eco-feminism. The role of Wangari Maathai in environmental conservation is recognized with emphasis on making efforts to embrace climate change to save Africa from the effects of climate change. While Gudhlanga, et al. also carries out a literary analysis to express ecological concerns, they do not underscore the pertinent role of Mother Nature in all spheres of life as is the subject of this book. Worse still, their scope is narrowed to Africa yet ecological issues are global in nature. Climate change does not just affect Africa, in fact mist, typhoons, earthquakes, and cyclones affect other continents such as Asia and North America.

1.3 The Statement of the Problem

This study transgresses the conventional tradition of highlighting ecological concerns in literary writing and instead shows how literary writers gives Mother Nature her rightful place. Using eco-criticism, the study challenges homocentric attributes of literature and underscores the impact of the ecological environment. This analytical study is, therefore, a close textual reading of the primary and secondary texts while L. Buell (2005) serves as a theoretical framework for the interpretation.

In this study I interrogate the influence of the ecological environment on desirable and undesirable cultural traditions in selected works of prose fiction, analyse the nexus between ecological environment and political systems in selected works of prose fiction, investigate the influence of ecological environment on religious aspects of characters in selected novels and finally analyse the nexus between ecological environment and historical events such as slavery, colonialism, scientific and industrial revolution in selected works of prose fiction.

In this first chapter, I have placed the study in context by expounding on the important voices related to the topic and how the study find its gap. There is a cogent justification of the study and elaborate statement of the problem. In Chapter Two, I will show how the ecological environment compels communities to choose certain cultural practices in selected works of prose fiction. These customs and traditions may be desirable or undesirable to the contemporary society. The chapter will have at least four essays on literary works from Africa and beyond. In Chapter Three I demonstrate how the natural environment dictates the political structures of societies in selected works of prose fiction. I will interrogate the role of Mother Nature on the choice of systems of government such as autocracy, democracy, aristocracy and monarchy in contemporary novels. The chapter will have at least three sub chapters to give adequate evidence. In chapter Four, I focus on the nexus between the ecological environment and religious aspects of characters in selected works of prose. The subchapters demonstrate how Mother Nature influences traditional religions in selected works of prose. The chapter will have four essays; at least one essay should be based on a work out of Africa. In Chapter five, I show the effect of Mother Nature on mental health issues. As much as mental illness is mostly related to human aspects such as othering and heredity, in this chapter I will investigate the role of the ecological environment in madness and the fragmented self. The Last Chapter, six, will have summaries, conclusions and research findings. The impact of Mother Nature on different facets of human life will be assessed according to the evidence gathered from the different chapters. New areas for future studies will be stated in the chapter.

REFERENCES

Bacon F. (1620). *The Novum Organum.* https://www.metaphysicspirit.com/books/The%20New%20Orga non.pdf.

Brueggemann, W 1989, Finally Comes The poet: daring speech for proclamation. Minneapolis: Fortress Press.

Buell, L. (2005). *The Future of Environmental Criticism: environmental Crisis and Literary Imagination.* Malden. MA: Blackwell Publishing.

Devall, W and Sessions, G. (1985). Deep Ecology: Living as if Nature Mattered, Salt Lake City: Gibbs M. Smith

Kamanzi, A. (2011). Modernity: foundation for universal environmental degradation, in *Journal of the College* of Humanities and Social Sciences: 10 .3: p. 204 – 213.

Mill, J.S. (1861, 1957) *Utilitarianism.* Indianapolis: Bobbs Merrill.

Spedding, J. Ellis, R.L., and Health, D.D (1970) eds, Bacon's Works, vol. 4, London: Longman's 14 Green

Chapter Two

Mother Nature and Social Spectrum: Class and Traditions in Contemporary Novels

People in different cultures learn specific behaviours in order to adapt to their environment. Even the same general skill will take on different forms, depending on unique environmental features and demands.

Lewis A. (2015)

The homocentric approach towards life tends to deride essential causes of human behaviour and in turn focus on peripheral issues such as gender inequalities and political factors. As much as human weaknesses determine human behaviour, scholars single out the role of heredity and environment as major determinants of human conduct. It is along this line that Lewis (2015) underscores the pertinent role of ecological environment particularly through the mention of "unique environmental features" (76). Lewis' reference to environmental adaptation underscores Mother Nature's superiority to humankind because she maintains her constitution and it is upon her subordinates (humankind, animals and plants) to change and live according to her desires. According to Lewis, culture is the sum total of behaviour learnt through adaptation to the environment. This suggests that different environments produce different cultural attributes as people try to adapt to their varying demands. Lewis insists that "learning is the mechanism through which the environment exerts its most profound effects on behaviour" (77). In short, the ecological environment will compel humankind to learn certain economic and social activities and customs. For example, we do not expect people living in arid areas to have rain makers because it rarely rains anyway. Furthermore, Mother Nature reinforces choice of economic activities that eventually determine the social condition of people. A region endowed with mineral resources such gold will obviously have better material condition than one solely depends of nomadism or peasantry.

As stated earlier, this chapter focuses on how the ecological environment compels characters to choose certain cultural and economic practices in selected works of prose fiction. The customs and traditions may be desirable or undesirable to the contemporary society, but the demands of Mother Nature compel humanity to do it. The chapter will have at least three subchapters on literary works from Africa and beyond. In the chapter, I investigate the role of Mother Nature on the class and cultural rites such as female circumcision, patriarchy and male chauvinism, poaching and raiding, early and forced marriages. These texts are Farah's *From the Crooked Rib*, Kyalo Mativo's *On the Market Day*, Mohamed's *Black Mamba Boy* and John Steinbeck's *The Pearl*.

Mother Nature and Social Condition: Violence and Migrancy in Nadifa Mohamed's *Black Mamba Boy* and Nyongesa's "The Sordid Boon"

> The Root cause of political strife and migration in Somalia is Italian colonial heritage beginning with the occupation that took longer than other African nations.
>
> Hess R. (1966)

Migrancy has become a culture in most communities in the world over, particularly in African Nations. Press reports about Africans from Nigeria, Eritrea and Somalia are broadcast day by day which has prompted scholars from different fields to account for the menace. Most scholars give homocentric reasons without any attempt to analyse ecological causes. It is this homocentric school that Hess (1966) underscores by singling out political strife and colonial heritage as the foundations if Somalis' penchant for migration. Hess avers that De Vecchi carried out the conquest with brutality that left severe scars on the Somali populace. The commissioner at Obbla, a Fascist colonel, would brood no insubordination on the part of the Somali sultan, effecting the occupation with such brutality that left indelible wounds on the Somali community (152); apparently, the political violence is mimicry of the colonial master. This subchapter investigates the role of Mother Nature in cultural aspects of characters including violence, migrancy, naming, and poverty, hunger, premature death, and sicknesses.

As much colonialism contributes to these cultural aspects of Somalia, an ecological reading of Mohamed's *Black Mamba Boy*, however suggests that there is a nexus between Mother Nature and the violence, migrancy and other traditions that have formed the cultural landscape of Somalia. Mohamed's Black *Mamba Boy* is a story of Jama Guure who struggles against the Onslaught of Mother Nature to earn, find his dream. Denied the right to a healthy childhood, Jama struggles to survive as street urchin in Aden, Yemen after his father abandons them in Hargeisa for lack of sustenance. Her baby sister Kawaharis dies of heat and thirst, which prompts Guure to depart to Sudan in search for a Job. Without a husband to care for her, Jama's mother, Ambaro migrates to Yemen in search for a job, where she catches illness and dies leaving Jama, a helpless orphan. He returns to his ancestral land, Hargeisa and then sets off from a small village in Hargeisa in the hope that he will succeed. Jama detests the harsh weather conditions of Hargeisa that have resulted in indigence among her relatives. Jama, therefore journeys to Eritrea, Sudan, Egypt, Palestine and ends up in the United Kingdom. Although he did not find his father, the briefcase he inherits from him becomes a supernatural aid that leads him to self-actualization. The spirit of his father saves him from the British airpower in Eritrea and leads him to Sudan where he prospers in farming and business. The locusts destroy his crops and he has to leave for Egypt where his father guides him to become a sailor.

Throughout the novel, Mohamed refers to the ecological environment as the trigger of Jama's migration from his Motherland, Hargeisa. Of Hargeisa, Jama says:

> Heat simmered above the ground, making the sparse vegetation look like a mirage that would fade away if you reached out for it. The emptiness of the desert felt purifying and yet disturbing after a tumultuous humanity of Aden. Deserts were birth places of prophets, but also playgrounds of jinnis and shape shifters. (49)

This passage shows how the constant spread desertification in Hargeisa, which Jama compares to Aden. There is less humanity in Hargeisa because the indigent conditions that ecological environment has caused. Jama revokes the image of "emptiness" in Hargeisa which signifies death or eradication of life. Indeed he witnesses poverty in Hargeisa as he cannot find a job as was his experience in Aden. He describes Hargeisa as a "barren town for places to work" because "shops and homes operated on the most basic levels of survival and there was no room for luxuries such as paid servants" (56). It is apparent that unlike what Spending et. al's claim about Nature being humankind's slave, (p.20) she has completely vanquished humanity and controlled every aspect of life in Hargeisa. This reiterates Cleaver and Schreiber (1994)'s views that livelihoods of the poor in desertification-prone areas are closely tied to the fate of their land; hence poverty and land degradation create a self-reinforcing downward spiral" (10). Poverty becomes endemic with more instances of desertification and this is the plight of Jama's parents when the drought sets in.

The narrator says, "[f]inally, when the drought decimated the clan's camels, sheep and goats, everything disintegrated and families dissolved as people sought survival down every dirt track" (22). In this passage, Mohamed suggests that the ecological environment wields enormous power as it determines many cultural elements in Jama's society. First, they cannot grow crops, but solely depend on pastoralism. Mohamed in this passage echoes Hess assertions that Agronomist Romolo Onor, who was invited to research on the agricultural potential of Somalia, got gravely depressed and committed suicide in 1918 (p.114). Unlike Kenya where the area around Mount Kenya was found to be agriculturally viable, the ecological conditions of Somalia rendered her terribly devoid of Agricultural potential.

Secondly, Mother Nature "dissolved families" which means, single parent family menace. Jama's father, Guure invites his wife and says, "[e]ither I go and make a living for us or you do" (22). He therefore sets of to an unknown place to find a source of livelihood because of drought in the Motherland. This is why Hess thesis on homocentric causes of migration runs counter to actual causes of migrancy in Somalia. Mohamed writes, "Guure set off on a mapless, penniless journey to Sudan. That was the last, they saw him, though they heard of his wanderings" (22). Jama's mother, Ambaro becomes a single mother and also resolves to leave for Aden to find a job. The reference to "wanderings" and "dirt track" connotes negative aspects of migrancy that include joblessness, desperateness and misery that may come with it.

Indeed, having escaped the onslaught of Nature at home, Somali immigrants in Aden occupy the lowest stratum of society. With her dear son, Jama, Ambaro lives in an abandoned warehouse. Jama says, "[s]leeping on roofs and streets had changed sleep pattern…to jerky half-awake unconsciousness" (23). One cultural practice that develops among Somali parents in Aden is parental negligence, which dominates contemporary families. Although Smith and Fong point out "psychopathy and cognitive distortions" (cited from Avdibegovic and Brkic, 2020, p.337 as the main cause of child neglect, Daniel et. al take the trajectory taken by this study when they aver that the "cause of neglect is in the interaction of family characteristics and environmental factors" (Avdibegovic and Brkic, 337). Ambaro and fellow Somali parents have fled an ecological disaster in Somaliland and end up as Mother Nature's refugees in Yemen. They spend all days slaving for Arabs to make their ends meet; Jama and other children of immigrant's live lonely lives. During the day, Jama roamed the street alone, and upon return to the "earth smelling crook on the roof of a teetering apartment block" (23), he would not miss his mother. Because she was always grumpy and quarrelsome in his presence, the narrator says the mother "did nothing but give him a headache" (23). Occasionally, immigrant women fight before their children and they start imbibing violence from their bitter parents. Ambaro fights with Dhegdheer, a fellow immigrant in front of children and they get involved to defend their mothers (16-17). Henceforth, Jama acquires propensity for violence. He joins a group of other neglected Somali boys to roam in Aden. The narrator says, "[t]heir fathers came and went regularly making money and losing it, with monsoon trade" (31). Having left Somalia, because of drought, to make money as sailors, they did not have time for children. With no parents to fear, "Somali boys saw the other children as well-fed and soft enough to harass safely" (31). If Somalia had conducive ecological environment, the parents would have settled and responsibly nurtured their children. But with constant search for an elusive livelihood, children are neglected; hence a savage generation.

While children in settler communities go to school, Jama and his colleagues, Abdi and Shidane loiter in Aden, "[l]ooking for boys their age to fight" (31). When they come across Jewish boys, Jama and his colleagues are so jealous of their good breeding and "Shidane picked up a stone and lobbed it at them" (32). Jama and Abdi did the same. While Jewish boys have books, which they try to protect from the intruders, Somali boys just have stones to throw at their age mates. In one of these wanderings, Jama and friends come across a woman who is being taken away to be stoned for prostitution. Abdi grabs the elder's cane and Jama bites the man's arm until he surrenders the cane (28). Although they save the woman, the children have acquired violent traits. Sometimes, the violence is extended to colleagues in the gang. When Jama gets a job at Mukhbazar and reports to Shidane and Abdi, the latter says that he does not need a bastard's help and terrible fight breaks out between them (37). When Abdi is overpowered, he picks his dagger and "plunged it deep into Jama's arm" (37). Shameful details are revealed about Abdi: her mother is a prostitute because the father was killed by a British mine. As a result, Abdi is a violent child; he hates his social condition. As much the father was killed by a

British mine, it would be absurd to link it to political causes without analysing the context. The British planted the mine during the Mad Mullah resistance to conquer the Somali for effective occupation (30). Ecological factors play an important part because the British came to Africa in search for raw materials. Mother Nature was a pull factor that caused colonial wars in Somalia and other African countries.

The condition of Somali children in Aden creates a class divide that makes them an easy target of othering. The narrator says, "[o]nly Somali children in Aden ran around feral, sleeping everywhere and anywhere. Many were children of single mothers working in office factories" (31). The single mother menace, as earlier pointed out, is not caused by premarital sex as is mostly asserted. Ambaro's marriage is dissolved by drought and she has to migrate to Aden to seek for a job. As they sleep in abandoned buildings and roam the city, Jewish children single them out and say, "[y]our fathers are dirty Somali punkawallahs" (32). It is clear that they are children of climate refugees and whose penchant for migration has denied them ability to raise well-bred children. The Jewish children are described as "prima and proper...overdressed with little skullcaps, balanced on their heads" (32). They go to school and demonstrate good behaviour.

On the other hand, Somali children have also acquired theft and begging as a result of ecological onslaught on their parents. When they are send away from the Jewish neighbourhood, Abdi steals a waistcoat and while in town, they storm into a hotel and steal spaghetti (p. 28-29). Jama opts for child labour because he was "was tired of always turning up a beggar at people's doors, begging for someone's leftover food, left over attention" (41). As much advent of modernity has inculcated more selfish traits in the people of Aden, Jama would not have ended up as a beggar if drought had not ended his family in Hargeisa.

In Nyongesa's *Sordid Boon,* characters are so much affected by the arid conditions in their area that clans precipitate violence against fellow clans over pastures. When Abdow takes his parents' pastures into the patch of grass designated for another clan, men ambush, torture and kill him. In his last reflections, he says:

> His people cleared all shrubs in Al-hamdu to burn charcoal and roamed with livestock over the little grass to pave way for unending droughts. Al Hamdu was a hot oven, a blazing hell that compelled them to sweat into the wee hours of the night. They did not need blankets to sleep at night. He had for the first time seen a blanket in Nyandarua. (51).

Abdow in this passage proves that ecological factors have reduced the dwellers of his town to the current state of indigence that provokes constant acts of violence. The environmental degradation in Al-hamdu is a process because of neglect thereby resulting in droughts that create clan conflicts. As much, as according to Abdow, poverty stands out as the major cause of violence, there is a suggestion that the high temperatures cause the heat stress that precipitates violence among personalities of desert dwellers.

According to Mullins and White (2019), "cold temperatures lead to decreases in the incidence of negative mental health outcomes and hot temperatures lead to [their] increases" (p. 2). The manner in which the antagonists treat Abdow demonstrates their pathological condition. Few minutes after arrest, one of the Marit clansman says, "[t]urn him prostrate...we beat then slaughter [...] and lynch this Kart as a warning to the rest" (50). They throw Abdow upside down and pummel him with all sorts of metals. The callous manner through which it is done is just blamed on the fact that Abdow hails from Kart, but has crossed over to the part of land belonging to the Marit. In his internal monologue, Abdow singles out the ecological hardships as the prime cause of violence in his community. He says "[t]ere were no pastures for livestock and when Allah brought some after the rains, his people killed each other over it and hence was his fate. For Abdow, the rain was a blessing and a curse. It was a sordid boon that brought death and life" (52). In this extract, the author transgresses Hess' insistence on blaming violence on political organization of Somali community. One of the major causes of clan conflicts among Somali people arises from ecological factors that cause savage competition for pastures and water. While Abdow expects to celebrate the advent of rainfall, one slip results in his torture and death.

The ecological environment also affects cultural rites such as naming and blessing of new-borns. The person's ability to succeed in life is said to be symbolized by the stars. According to Tedd Peters, this is astrotheology, of which focus is both "creation" and the deities (839). Peter's emphasis on creation is reference to the ecological environment and its contributions to the religious aspects of humanity. In Mohamed's *Black Mamba Boy*, Ambaro exhorts her son to look at the sky as the source of blessings for humanity. She says, "[l]ook at those stars Goode, they have watched everything ...and have power and meaning in life. That star tells us when to mate the sheep. If that one does not appear we should expect trouble that little leads us to the sea" (44). For Ambaaro, the Somali community is so steeped in astrotheology that the seasons for their economic activities are all determined by the stars in the sky. Mother Nature therefore guides community activities and creates logical meaning for interpretation of existence. According to Chami (2008), the Musi of Ethiopia also saw the sun as a "calender for religious, sailing and economic activities" (122). Similarly, nothing can take place smoothly in Somaliland without the spiritual invocation by these celestial bodies. For her, her son's star is associated with another creature in their ecology, the black mamba. After ordering his conception, the star sends a black mamba snake to caress the boy in the womb (12). That is why in spite of the father's refusal, she calls her Goode, the Black mamba. In Ambaro's opinion, the star associated with the Black mamba sanctioned his birth to be accompanied with fat worms on the earth, a rainy season which constitutes the "most beautiful lack" (13). Indeed in Jama's life, he turns out lucky in his endeavours.

When Jama's late sister is born, her name is given according to Mother Nature's dictates. She is beautiful, "a smiling golden eyes with big happy eyes" (21) and so Ambaro names her Hawaris, a Somali word for "the glow of light before sunrise" (21). This shows that in Ambaro's society, beauty, ugliness; success, failure; power and weakness are all associated with the ever present existence of superiority of Mother Nature. One can only be as successful as or beautiful as that which is symbolized by the ecological environment.

REFERENCES

Achami, F. (2008). Evidence of Ancient African Beliefs in Celestial Bodies. 121-130pp. https://link.springer.com/chapter/10.1007/978-1-4020-6639-9_10?noAccess=true.

Avdibegovic, E. and Brkic M. (2020). Child neglect- Causes and Consequences. *Psychiatra Dabumina*, 32: 337-342. https://www.psychiatria-danubina.com/UserDocsImages/pdf/dnb_vol32_noSuppl%203/dnb_vol32_noSuppl%203_337.pdf.

Cleaver, K. M. and Schreiber, G. A. (1994). Reversing the Spiral: The Population,

Agriculture and Environment Nexus in Sub-Saharan Africa. The World Bank, Washington, D.C.

Daniel B, Taylor J, Scott J: (2011). Recognizing and helping the neglected child: Evidence-based practice for assessment and intervention. London: Jessica Kingsley Publishers, 2011

Hess, R. (1966). *Italian Colonialism*. London: Chicago Press

Lewis A. (2015). Genes, environment and behaviour.

Smith MG, Fong R. (2004). The children of neglect: when no one cares. New York and Hove: Brunner-Routledge.

Mullins, J. T., & White, C. (2019). Temperature and mental health: Evidence from the spectrum of mental health outcomes. *Journal of Health Economics,* 102240 https://doi.org/10.1016/j.jhealeco.2019.102240

Nyongesa. A. (2021). The Sordid Boon. *The Armageddon and Other Stories: An Anthology of Short Stories from Africa.* Ed. Andrew Nyongesa and John Mugubi. Nairobi: Nsemia Inc. Publishers.

Tedd Peters. "Astrotheology". Chapter 72 of Routledge of Modern Christian Thought, ed. Chad Meister and James Beiby. London and New York: Routledge 2013. Pp.838-853.

Patriarchy and Infibulation: Mother Nature's Autocracy in Contemporary Novels

> In other words, the body of the woman is thought of as asexualized for the woman; she cannot experience any sexual pleasure with it. This is in sharp contradiction to man, who can find his sexual pleasure within and through the body of the woman and with his own body.
>
> Meriem H. (99)

Feminist critics have constantly associated infibulation among African communities with patriarchal attempt to asexualize the woman's body for the benefit of men. As earlier mentioned, feminist scholars have deliberately taken a homocentric approach towards infibulation with least attempt to consider the role of Mother Nature in the origin and perpetuation of the practice. The above quote by Merime is one of the many feminist sentiments that focus on a homocentric elements of feminism. This subchapter will investigate the effect of ecological factors in the invention of and perpetuation of female genital mutilation in Nyongesa's *Worms in the Lounge* and Farah's *From a Crooked Rib*.

Characters in the two literary texts deliberately points finger of calumny at patriarchal traditions as the major cause of infibulation without any attempt to consider the impact of ecological environment. According to Njogu and Orchardson-Mazrui (2013) some African communities that practiced crop farming embraced matrilineality, but patriarchy pervaded pastoralist communities (p. 4). The Somali, where *From the Crooked Rib* and *Worms in the Lounge* are set, are pastoralist communities hence the patriarchal tendencies that elevate female circumcision. Adarge (2014) asserts:

> FGM is thought to sustain and transfer traditions, to reduce girl's sexual desire and possible provocation which they believe unless a girl is circumcised she would ask men to have sex; and the fear for societal exclusion on parents and the possibility of a girl to be seen as shameful and less attractive for marriage. (p.5)

This quite attests to the patriarchal dominance among pastoral communities of which aim is to elevate men's sexuality and subdue female sexuality. These pastoral communities seem to be affected by women's propensity to desire to have sex. They describe this as a shameful and embarrassing attribute. It is interesting how Adarge describes the climatic conditions of her area of study as "flat landscape with arid climatic condition having low rain fall in most of its parts" (3) to confirm the prevalence of FGM in arid and semi- arid areas. Adarge argues that although communities living in wet areas of Ethiopia do carry out female circumcision, it is not as severe as the one practiced in Afar, which is an arid area. It is apparent that hostile ecological conditions elevate patriarchal traditions including female genital mutilation.

Indeed male characters in Nyongesa's *Worms in the Lounge* and Farah's *From a Crooked Rib* exhibit patriarchal tendencies that they have bequeathed from their ecological surroundings. As an adaptation to the hostile ecological conditions, Ebla's grandfather, in *From a Crooked Rib,* exhibits in human tendencies. He gives Ebla away to the forty-eight year old Giumeh without any attempt to inform Ebla. Grandfather does this because in the patriarchal community where he has grown up, "[g]irls were materials, just like objects or items on the shelf of a shop. They were sold and bought as shepherds sold their goats at market places" (p.37). Farah's mention of shepherds and goats is a deliberate reference to the nomadic pastoralism that works in conjunction with the hostile environment to effect commodification of girls and women.

Ebla lacks an emotional connection with her Grandfather because of his tendency to treat her like livestock. When her brother mentions Grandfather, Ebla can only say, "[h]e was a man- just like any other man. What was the difference? His wife (her grandmother) must have suffered his brutal man handlings" (44). Ebla suggests that Grandfather is a naturally violent and inhuman person. However, the environmental conditions must have compelled Grandfather to develop this kind of behaviour. Avis (2018) singles out a history of violence and trauma as one causes of inhumanity and violence among pastoralists (5). The competition for pastures and water cause armed conflicts that dehumanize men in the cause of time. Asha's father in Nyongesa's *Worms in the Lounge* exhibits similar traits. The narrator says, "[i]f Halima missed him then his children indeed hungered for his face. Sixth of his seven wives, Halima was a bit fortunate to have him twice in four months. Not that he hated his wives, Derrow Maalim Samatar was too footloose to dwell in one place" (57). Like Ebla's Grandfather, Derrow does not seem to value family life because of his propensity to disrespect women. The idea is to have a woman everywhere he resides as he migrates from one point of life to another. This migration is attributed to hostile ecological conditions that force nomads to search for greener pastures. Asha's brother, Yusuf tells Eugene, "[i]t is very hard to contain a nomad [...] they are always seeking for greener pastures and water" (222-223). The migration exposes women and girls to men from the so called "enemy" communities that puts their blood line at risk. Asha's father himself migrates from Mandera to different regions in East Africa. By ensuring that Asha has undergone genital cutting, he believes she is safer from these foreign men.

One thing that Asha has grown to know is her father's penchant for violence; the narrator says, "her father owned a gun and he knew she would appear ready for death. Members of her family had a penchant for fighting uncontrollably and in so doing were driven by emotions rather than reason" (80). Asha's father is in fact the family member whose desire to dominate women and "others" drives to exhibit feats of violence. He therefore hates men from other communities who try to talk to his daughters. Although he has migrated from his hot and dry area, Mandera, to Okoro (western Kenya), Derrow continues with this habit. When Asha stops to appreciate Tom for saving her from the hands of violent boys, Derrow accosts him with a pistol (81). Many questions are raised by the men's propensity to exaggerate any girl's interaction with men from other communities.

In the prologue of *Worms in the Lounge*, the Maalim (Duksi teacher) forbids girls from shaking hands with non-Somali men. He says, tells Asha and female pupils, "[y]ou want to talk like infidels, you want to greet like them...hey, you want to shake a boy's hand, ahem. A boy who is not your relative" (31). As much as the Maalim (Duksi teacher) purports to instil religious ideas, there is an underlying desire to stop intermarriage between Somali girls and Bantu communities living in Kenya.

It is also essential to investigate the cause of the perennial fear for intermarriage among the pastoralist communities. Kwaak et. al (2012) observe:

> When we look at nomadic communities, reproductive health is a crucial issue. The lifestyle of moving from place to place for subsistence seems to deprive nomadic communities from basic reproductive health services. (23)

Indeed migratory tendencies by pastoral communities affect their exposure to reproductive health. However, in this sub chapter, it is prudent to note that nomadic lifestyle exposes the girls and women to men from other communities, which to most Africa are considered "enemies". Stories about dangerous ogres told to girls were meant to discourage them from marrying into communities considered enemy to preserve the bloodline. If men migrated to different places and left women and girls in the hands of foreign communities, the girls would be impregnated and give birth to children not belonging to these communities. This is the major cause of heightened patriarchal dominance among the pastoralists aimed to protect the blood line from many dangers. It is no wonder early marriage, forced marriage and many children are cited as other are practices common among pastoralists (Kwaak, p.16). In spite of his criticism of the practice, Kulet (2017) demonstrates how enemy communities would raid Maasai people and exploit their women sexually in front of their husbands because of the women's inability to control their sexual desires. As a result, the community invented female circumcision for women to have control over their sexual desires. Indeed several passages in the two novels in this chapter show how female characters that have undergone infibulation detest sexual intercourse. In *Worms in the Lounge*, Asha says:

> Any mental picture of something approaching her groin sent reflex of fear up her nerves. The callous knife of the surgeon, the smarting stings it breathed and the pounding throbs it left around her private parts came back to her mind. Then followed the pangs that accompanied the repeat. The first operation had left a bean sized opening. The surgeon had then repeated the operation to refine it. A sorghum grain size is what she aimed at as she inserted the knife to sever off her meat […] it was not without tears that she afforded short call. Which sex could she enjoy having no instruments of passion? (p. 40-41)

Asha, in this passage, confirms that infibulation is a crude surgical operation aimed at mutilating the sexual organs of the girl to render her incapable of having sex particularly with men from other communities. The small opening that can hardly allow menstruation will completely put off any man that is not used to this kind of rite. The traumatic memories of the experience renders Asha incapable of appreciating sex and she keeps away from young men with feelings for her. Although she may be willing to enjoy some intimacy with her boyfriend, Eugene. To prevent Asha from intermarriage is basically the major aim of female genital cutting because besides being unable to have sex with young men from other communities, her father Derrow consistently becomes a stumbling block for such relationships. When he learns of the bond of affection between Asha and Tom, Derrow tricks her with an invitation to pay them a visit to Mandera only for Asha to realize that it is a ploy to apprehend and marry her forcefully to Abdirahman Derrow Samatar. Because of his Bantu origin, Tom is deliberately otherized at the event. Asha says:

> Four men shot out of the hotel [...]. With Tom, we moved towards them. They received my hand happily but frowned at Tom's hand. I retreated and insisted on stepping inside on condition that Tom was permitted. As Tom, an outcast in the present circumstances, I recalled his godly acts of generosity and commitment to restoration of my dignity. I let my tears flow. (p. 211)

As much as Asha knows how supportive and instrumental Tom has been to his education and future, the members of his family see him as an outcast because he does not belong to her community. The men enforce a physical separation between Tom and their daughter to execute the aims of female circumcision. When Tom tries to wipe away Asha's tears, the Somali men say, "[d]on't touch her" (212) and shove Asha away to a specified hotel.

Similarly, although Ebla in *From a Crooked Rib* does not come in contact with non-Somali men, she experiences challenges in her sex life because of infibulation. On the first night with her boyfriend Awill, the narrator says:

> Ebla was very frightened, not of Awill, but because she was a virgin. She had heard lots of women talking about the pain one undergoes when one has one's first sexual intercourse. She had been circumcised when she was eight: the clitoris had been cut and stitched. She wished more than anything else that she was not a woman. She remembered Aowralla's painful child-delivery when she was in Belet Wene. (p.42)

Like Asha in *Worms in the Lounge,* the operation involves cutting of outer parts of the female sexual organ and stitching to control the girl's sexual behaviour. The dread that Ebla has is same as that that Asha exhibits. The elders in the community do not have to struggle watching over the girls because they have already instituted a biological mechanism to hinder sexual interaction. The pain such women experience during sexual intercourse serves as a deterrent and so they cannot have love relationships with foreign men. Ebla wishes she was not a woman now that even giving birth is so painful. Although virginity is viewed as a symbol of purity, it is also reinforced by a stitch to put off men from other communities. This is evident in the story of Zeitun Kassim in *Worms in the Lounge*. Tom is surprised when Zeitun informs him that her father "insists that I should be a virgin in spite of being a divorcee. Oh darling, have you ever heard of a divorcee who is virgin?" (p.184). Zeitun reveals that although she is not a virgin, her father compelled her to undergo a surgery and have synthetic virginity. When Tom woos Zeitun to bed, the virginity puts him off. He says:

> Like any normal man curious to taste a new dish, I wooed her into my bed. The result was an embarrassment. She hardly possessed the tools of passion. I saw something like a pinhole. Any attempt to penetrate it was not only rape but also self-torture. Believe you me; my small finger could hardly get through her birth canal. (p. 185)

The profound shock that follows Tom's experience compels him to leave Zeitun alone as she delves into how virginity has been used to conceal hypocrisy among nomadic communities. The mutilated and stitched female organ looks strange and becomes familiar to those men from the girl's community because they understand the crudity of the cultural rite.

It is apparent that the patriarchal tradition is so intense among nomadic communities of Africa because of the fear among men that they would lose their bloodline to 'enemy' communities given their tendency to migrate from one place to another. The girl is so firmly controlled and all decisions are made for her. Ebla for instance says, "[i]f a woman is slept with a man, her relations either shot her or knifed her to death," (43). This means the men in the community had full rights over the girls' bodies. The girls could not control their bodies just to ensure that only children from the target community are sired. This is a belief that Asha questions in *Worms in the Lounge*. The patriarchal regimentation reduces her into a marionette:

> She was tired. Asha would have liked to live like families in Okoro. In her family everything was dictated at her. She had grown up as a recipient of decisions made by grown-ups. Yes was the automatic response to every idea that came. Asha had to obey countless commands. 'Who was their author?' she asked herself. 'Why must always obey them?' Even such thoughts were said to be sin. Asha Derrow was a bucket to receive water, a pit latrine to receive diarrhoea, hard stools and dysentery without question. (p.74)

In this passage, the patriarchal dominance ensures that girls such as Asha cannot make any decisions for themselves. The community thinks for them, and they are forced to obey everything they are told. The authors of these laws are male elders who have no touch with the realities affecting women and girls. Girls are therefore "pit latrines" that passively receive decisions made by men. This is a similar situation that Ebla faces in *From a Crooked Rib* because Grandfather makes a decision to who she ought to marry (9). When she runs away to her cousin's home at Belet Wene, he dictates her marriage to the sick broker Dirir (14). Ebla's cousin Gheddi is a very imposing figure and sometimes makes decisions without consulting the wife. He blames Ebla as the source of misfortune and when his wife Aowralla disagrees with him, he says he would hit her (29). When she reaches Mogadicio, elders such as Asha and Tiffo, conspire to make all decisions for Ebla concerning private matters that she should make her own decisions.

These are the same complaints that Asha raises in *Worms in the Lounge* when she compares a Somali girl to an egg. She says "the poor egg could not think for itself; it could not decide the best place for incubation" (113). The farmer makes all decisions for the well-being of the eggs and so is Asha's plight. Men make all decisions for girls and women. Asha asks, "[h]ow can I count myself as an achiever if Father chooses for me the school, clothes, friends, books, leisure, neighbours, food, all the way to a husband? I am too foolish to choose anything?" (p.114). The father represents the patriarchal regimented order that controls women to protect the bloodline from the so called enemy communities.

REFERENCES

Adarge M. (2014). The Difficulties of Ending Female Genital Mutilation (FGM): Case of Afar Pastoralist Communities in Ethiopia: Case of Afar Pastoralist Communities in Ethiopia. *International Institute of Social Studies*. https://www.ohchr.org/sites/default/files/Documents/Issues/Women/WRGS/FGM/NGOs/ActionForIntegratedSustainableDevelopmentAssociation.pdf.

Amis W. (2018). Rebuilding pastoralist livelihoods during and after conflict. K4D. https://opendocs.ids.ac.uk/opendocs/bitstream/handle/20.500.12413/14259/421 Rebuilding Pastoralist Livelihoods During and After Conflict.

Farah, N. (1970). *From a Crooked Rib*. New York: Pengun Books

Kwaak et. al (2012). Understanding Nomadic Realities: Case studies on sexual and reproductive health and rights in Eastern Africa. KIT publishers: https://www.kit.nl/wp-content/uploads/2019/03/2009_LR_understanding_nomadic_realities.pdf.

Nyongesa, A. (2012). *Worms in the Lounge*. Nairobi. Splendour Publication Agencies.

Mother Nature, Human Behaviour and Livelihoods: Economic Practices in John Steinbeck's *The Pearl* and Mativo's "On the Market Day"

> In general, education—as a critical component of a country's human capital—increases the efficiency of each individual worker and helps economies to move up the value chain beyond manual tasks or simple production processes (WEF 2016). Human capital has long been considered the most distinctive feature of the economic system and further work has proven the impact of education on productivity growth empirically.
>
> Grant (2017, p.2)

Scholars have singled out many factors that influence the economic live of communities including education levels and technological potential of the nation. Industrialized nations such as The United

States, China, Japan and Great Britain peg their economic success on industrialisation and technological advancements. This is the argument that Grant advances in the above quote because she takes a homocentric approach that does not consider the role of the ecological environment. For Grant, what governments should seek in the pursuit of economic success is empowerment of citizens with skills, competences and knowledges rather than invest in conservation of the ecological environment.

This subchapter overturns Grants' argument and underscores the need to conserve the ecological environment as part and parcel of economic empowerment of citizens with reference to Steinbeck's *The Pearl* and Kyalo Mativo's "On the Market Day." It is the contention of this subchapter that some skills and competences gained in the education process become subservient to Mother Nature as some educated persons come in to mitigate the effects of the ecological environment.

Steinbeck's *The Pearl* is a story of Kino, a fisherman who lives in abjection and is constantly otherized by his affluent neighbours until he is lucky to find a pearl in the oysters at sea. His knowledge of the oysters and how they had produced pearls to change the lives of many in Spain and Europe prompts him to be constant search at sea. His search pays off when he finds the great pearl of the world and his former rivals come streaming to his house including the doctor, the priest and neighbours to serve and get something from Kino. Mativo's "On the market Day" is the story of Kamali Lango, a livestock trader whose flock in cattle is devastated by a severe drought and resorts to trading in livestock to make a living. To save his family from famine, Lango wakes up in the morning for a journey to the market to buy a cow for sell for profit. Obsessed by rare optimism, he spends all his five year savings to buy a cow, but on the way back home, the long trek on the scorching sun results on the death of the cow. Lango loses his business and returns empty handed to his wife and mother in-law awaiting his financial support. The vivid description of story's setting confirms the effect of ecological factors to the economic fortunes of Lango's community. With firm optimism and determination, Lango endures the hot sun, hunger and thirst by trekking all the way, but just as he approaches the market, his cow collapses and dies. Lango has to return to his poor family without any means of livelihood.

Mativo and Steinbeck negate the homocentric approach to underscore the role of ecological factors in the economic lives of characters. Kino's economic fortunes are tied to the ecological environment he has grown up. Steinbeck writes:

> Light filtered down through the water to the bed where the frilly pearl oysters lay fastened to the rubbly bottom, a bottom strewn with shells of broken, opened oysters. This was the bed that had raised the King of Spain to be a great power in Europe in past years, had helped pay for his wars, and had decorated the churches for his soul's sake. The grey oysters with ruffles like skirts on the shells, the barnacle-crusted oysters with little bits of weed clinging to the skirts and small crabs climbing over them. [...] for

> centuries, men had dived down and torn the oysters from their beds and ripped them open, looking for coated grains of sand. Swarms of fish lived near the bed to live near the oysters thrown back by searching men to nibble at the shining inner shells. But pearls were accidents and finding of one was luck, a little backed by God or the gods or both. (p. 34)

In this extract, Steinbeck underscores the superiority of the sea to the economic and human conduct of characters. This physical feature has immensely affected the lives of people by providing means of livelihood, shaping their social visions and affecting their system of beliefs. Kino suggests that the sea and its contents has invented political careers, elevated and stretched their influences to international levels. He mentions the King of Spain and his great influence as one such an example. Other economic activities include fishing for the "swarms of fish" near the bed of the river. The majority are peal finders who plough through the oysters day by day to find pearls to sell. Trading is therefore established in Kino's community and professionals such as medics have to come to the town to treat those that get injured in the search for fish and pearls. Steinbeck's argument concurs with Everett (2010) who assert:

> The natural environment plays an important role in supporting economic activity. It contributes directly, by providing resources and raw materials such as water, timber and minerals that are required as inputs for the production of goods and services; and • indirectly, through services provided by ecosystems including carbon sequestration,

water purification, managing flood risks, and nutrient cycling. Natural resources are, therefore, vital for securing economic growth and development, not just today but for future generations. (p. 7)

Everett et. al acknowledge the role of Mother Nature in laying foundation of the economic well-being of the community in terms of the raw materials and favourable ecosystem for production. Kino's community cannot produce pearls, fish and other water products without the enormous presence of the Sea and its contents. The activities that take place in the exploitation of the sea influence many economic activities including the professionals in the area. To facilitate fishing, craftsmen have to make canoes and boats and acquire skills to repair them in case. Of the canoe, the narrator says "was one thing of value he owned. [...] it was at once a property and source of food, for a man with a boat can guarantee a woman that she will eat something" (p. 32). This is the same way Nature influences the choice of economic activities in Kamali Lango's community in "On the Market Day."

The hot and dry climate has diminished any hopes for crop growing and Lango's people opt for cattle rearing and trade. In an internal monologue, Lango thinks:

> He lost how many cattle? .... ' The spotted one, the sharp-horned heifer, the brown bull, the white-crowned cow, the black-topped ... . .the .. ... ; that's all. Or? . .•. Yeah, that's all. Nevertheless.... 'Nevertheless, that's what he means, the sun always rises "even if not always to the Glory of God."

This year, if all goes well, 'I mean if the rains fall ....,' he paused for a while to endure the agonizing memory. 'There used to be a thick forest here, saturated with life... and now all that remains is dry whirlwind ..... Anyway this year if the rains come I could make as much as, ooh, two hundred, three hundred ... (p. 269)

Through this internal monologue, it is clear that Lango is a pastoralist because the dictates of the ecological setting. The ecological conditions do not permit him to grow crops such as coffee, tea, pyrethrum and other cash crops that other Kenyans grow to sell for a livelihood. In spite of the effort to keep the cattle, the persistent droughts cause massive losses, for example the previous year alone, he lost five head of cattle, "' The spotted one, the sharp-horned heifer, the brown bull, the white-crowned cow, the black-topped ..." His inability to name them as it happens in other communities in Kenya suggests that Lango is illiterate. The economic circumstances have undoubtedly dictated his educational status. Caged by the ecological to an indigent existence, trade becomes the sole means of making money, but his lack of formal education limits his entrepreneurial skills. Lango's plight cannot be separated from the humankind's neglect of Mother Nature that provides the basic necessities of life. The reference to the forest that was, but is now missing suggests the homocentric culture that has neglected Mother Nature. The environmental degradation, Mativo suggests, is caused by human activity, which reiterates Bacon' claims. In his *New organ*, he writes:

> Man, being the servant and interpreter of Nature, can do and understand so much and so much only as he has

observed in fact or in thought of the course of nature. Beyond this he neither knows anything nor can do anything. (I)

In Lango's community, the people are reckless interpreters of Mother Nature since they cut down trees in attempt to invert the master-servant norm to occupy Mother Nature's position. But Mother Nature has determinately occupied her position to prove them wrong through constant droughts, dust and heat that result in death of livestock to cause indigence and famine. For Bacon, humankind has surrendered their claim to superiority and remain servants of Mother Nature to maintain that benevolent interdependence. Servants, as is widely known, are experts to invent lofty ideas to serve masters, but focus on the small things that make their master happy. This is the one thing that Mativo satirises in aspiring Member of Parliament, Pancreas Mbula. When one elder asks him what he will do to mitigate the effects of drought, he gives lofty scientific solutions to assert his homocentric attitude, which has caused the current problem. He tells the elderly man:

> Now, right now we are sitting on a pool of water, and on both sides we are flanked by two perennial rivers. Lift up your eyes," he said, pointing away, "do you all see that mountain towering above the clouds with a white cap on top of it? Well, that 'cap' is actually a frozen lake whose water melts four times every year and trickles down the mountain-sides right through the thick forest surrounding it, zigzagging its way down the slopes. Now, four times melted water is equal to twice as much water again as we receive from natural rain. Indeed with that much water we

can turn this semi-desert into a green field all year round. And we have the will and the energy for that ." (p.273).

Mbula does not refer to any steps he would take to serve Mother Nature for example planting trees and limiting deforestation; instead he elevates homocentric efforts that would uphold environmental degradation by cutting down more trees to sink boreholes and irrigation dykes for crop farming. What he does not tell the people is that increased human activity (irrigation projects and trade) will increase carbon dioxide in the area and the subsequent global warming will eradicate the ice cap and render his project null and void in less than a decade. Why does Mbula evade the simple service to humanity such as planting trees? Must one resort to winding explanations as solution to persistent droughts when a lasting solution is within reach? It boils down to humankind's claim to Mother Nature's rightful position: Master or Mistress that is revealed at the end of his speech, "[w]hoever doubts that doubts the power of the people" (p. 273). Mbula, like his contemporaries, have gone through modern education, which underscores the invincibility of humanity over Mother Nature. But what Lango experiences is not in tandem with what they believe. His life confirms that the people are under the onslaught of Mother Nature.

Lango's mantra, for instance proves Mother Nature's superiority over humanity. As he walks along the path he has used the previous five years, Lango says, "[t]he sun always rises, even if not always to the Glory of God" (p. 269).The sun represents the hostile ecological conditions that have debilitated the economic muscles of Lango's community, such that everyone is aware of it. On the way, Lango observes the hostility of Mother Nature:

> The naked sun rose slowly and surely, an accursed red ball of ill-will. For days on end, it had risen in the same manner behind the same mountain. Sure enough, another daybreak. And there, all around him, rose a sea of dust, stretching far and beyond the sky-line. It was a familiar sight and the man had long ceased to take note of it. His feet, covered with red soil, carried him triumphantly as they had always done for countless times before. (p. 271)

The orb of the sun is a red ball that has devastated the lives of many a creature in this community for many years in spite of their claim to the Master or mistress position. Besides the heat that saps energy from animals and people, there is dust that poses a health risk to the populace. In a literary sense, the dust signifies death that threatens the lives of the inhabitants in this area. The magnitude of the dust "stretching far and beyond the skyline" demonstrates the extend of environmental degradation and its potential to limit the economic foresight of Lango and his contemporaries. Their region has been neglected by the government, partly because of its low economic potential. There are no roads and Lango has to walk long distances to the cattle market. The narrator clarifies that "his feet carried him triumphantly as they had always done for countless times before." Whereas people in other communities board public transport to rush to the market, buy cattle and use Lorries to transport them to markets, Lango has to trek long distances with his cow. According Ian Heggie (2022), limited resources prompt African countries to compel them to "restore only those roads that are economically justified" (1). In other words, the Kenyan government cannot prioritize road construction in areas that have low economic potential such as Lango's area because of hostile ecological conditions. As a result, people who resort to trade in the area suffer terrible losses.

Kamali Lango treks for many kilometres with his cow on the hot sun; the narrator says "Lango will stay with a friend of his mid-way between the buying and the selling market. By sunset tomorrow he will have arrived at the selling market" (p. 276). This suggests that Lango will trek twelve hours on the hot sun with his cow to the market. The experience is not as simple as he imagines because Mother Nature is braced for a decisive onslaught. Indeed the following day Mother Nature proves herself as the mistress to be dreaded. The narrator says:

> They walked all day, the man and the animal, until they were both exhausted by the heat. So they decided to stop under a tree for a short rest. He tied the animal to a nearby twig and lay down for a small nap. The quietness of the place lulled him into a deep sleep. How long it had lasted he couldn't quite tell. And when he woke up the animal was still there, but this time it was also lying down. (p. 276)

Both the trekking and the heat, which emanate from the hostile climatic conditions contribute to the exhaustion of Lango and his bull. When he wakes up all his attempt to raise the animal that embodied his life savings become an exercise in futility. "The animal remained immobile. He hit it harder. Still the animal didn't move. He grabbed its ears and pulled them" (276). The bull is possibly dehydrated because the writer does not tell the reader any watering point they visited throughout the twelve hour journey. When Lango canes the bull, it collapse, kicks in the air, groaned and "there was silence" (p. 277). Lango returns to his home at Kamulamba having lost all his working capital for the last five years.

Whereas Mother Nature diminishes Kamali Lango's fortunes directly in Mativo's "On the Market Day", she does the same indirectly in Steinbeck's *The Pearl*. The presence of the sea prompts Kino and fellow villagers to take astute fishing and exploration to find pearls with delusional hopes of attaining a status akin to the king of Spain. The Sea enables him to find the pearl and word travels like bushfire to all friend and foe concerning Kino's new status. The narrator says that before Kino and his wife Juana reach the brush house, "the nerves of the town were...vibrating with the news—Kino had found the pearl of the world" (p. 41). While Mother Nature compels Lango in Mativo's "On the market Day" to tend pride through unparalleled optimism, in Steinbeck's *The Pearl*, Nature nurtures Kino's pride through greed and constant flatter that comes with false comfort of being rich.

Within a few days of finding the pearl from the Sea, Kino's mind is transformed towards the path of self- destruction. Lofty ideas start filling his mind:

In the pearl, he saw Juana and Coyotito and kneeling at the high altar and they were being married now that they could pay. He spoke softly: we will be married – in church. In the pearl he saw how they were dressed – in the shawl stiff with newness and new skin and from under the long skirt Kino could see that she wore shoes. It was the pearl– the picture glowing there…he himself was dressed in new white clothes, and he carried a new hat- not of straw but of fine black felt. " (p. 44)

Kino no longer has the humility and sobriety he had after Mother Nature gives him access to the pearl. He is now that very important person to marry decently at the altar, speak in gentle tones, dress decently and become conscious of his security. Kino puffs up gradually and starts contemplating owning a rifle. In his current affluent state, "it was a rifle that broke down the barriers" (p. 45), to distinguish him from the poor. Kino no longer identifies with the poor with whom he had lived all his life. He craves for class distinction and now wants his son to receive formal education. He thinks, "[m]y son will open books, my son will write and will know writing" (p.46). This is reference to selfish ambition at the expense of the good of his society. Another change Juana realized in Kino's life is his readiness to murder when a thief appears in the house to steal the pearl. Juana is confounded when "Kino's hand crept into his breast where his knife hung …then he sprang like an angry cat…striking and spitting for the dark thing he knew was in the dark corner of the house" (58). He who had not confronted violence before now finds "warm blood running down from his forehead" (p.59) without any qualms. Several instances of animosity appear in succession after the family's possession of the pearl, which dull Kino's conscience. Before the family's departure, thieves make another incursion and Kino "got his knife out and lunged at one dark figure" (p. 84). Kino's wife Juana is confounded at her husband's evil act of killing the man. "A dead man in the path and Kino's knife, dark-bladed beside him" (p.85). It is Juana tasked with the responsibility of dragging the dead from the pathway into the shelter" (p.86). Kino's tragic fall comes when he journeys away from home in search for pearl buyer and is besieged by trackers and in the ensuing spurt of violence, he murders several men. Out of desire to possess the pearl, (the treasures of Mother Nature), Kino possesses a rifle from a tracker and "struck the head of the man like a melon" (p. 115). Kino's inhumanity is explicated by the narrator when he says "Kino had become as cold and deadly as steel" (115), but before this the tracker had mistaken Coyotito's cry for a coyote and shot. Kino and Juana return home having lost the child, the sole link between their present and future.

Bradbury E. (1968) observes that the pearl has varied significance:

> The pearl itself is loaded with symbolisms. One may see the pearl as symbolic of greed, beauty, materialism, freedom from want, evil, good, a spent and wasted society, degenerate religion, unethical medicine. (p.19).

This study views the pearl as a symbol of materialism, because Mother Nature provides material objects that trigger greed in Kino's heart. In his attempt to use what the ecological environment had given him, Kino loses his ethical values and worse still his only son, who is a link between him and posterity. As much as critics point out personal weaknesses as the cause of Kino's downfall, the presence of the Sea cannot be taken for granted as it provides the oysters and pearls to tempt Kino. Steinbeck implies that the ecological environment has the potential to shape people's personalities.

REFERENCES

Bradbury E. (1968). A Study of the Symbolism in Three Novels of John Steinbeck: To A God Unknown, The Pearl, and The Winter of Our Discontent. *Morehead State Theses and Dissertations. 216.* https://scholarworks.moreheadstate.edu/msu_theses_dissertations/216

Heggie, I. G. (2022). Management and Financing of Roads. World bank technical paper number 275 Africa technical series. https://www.ssatp.org/sites/ssatp/files/publications/WorldBank-TechnicalPapers/TP275/TP275.pdf.

Grant C. (2017). The contribution of education to economic growth. *Institute of Development Studies.* *https://assets.publishing.service.gov.uk/media/5b9b87f340f0b67896977bae/K4D_HDR_The_Contribution_of_Education_to_Economic_Growth_Final.pdf.*

Steinbeck. J. (2000). The Pearl. Essex: Pearson Education LTD.

Chapter Three

Mother Nature and Politics: Ecological Attributes and Governance

Communities the world over associate leadership styles to the creativity, cultural and social organisation of a people. In some instances, individuals have been credited for introduction of political systems such as democracy in particular nations. In Africa, Nelson Mandela has been credited for introduction of democracy in South Africa. Thomas Jefferson has been credited as the Father of Modern democratic United States and Mao Tse Dung the father of Modern Communist (dictatorship) China. But to what extent is this homocentric approach true? To what extent does the ecological setting influence the governance styles adopted by different communities the world over? In his view about the rise of democracy in Africa, Sesay (2014), writes:

> African nationalists rejected the authoritarian traditional governance systems in favour of democracy even before independence in the 1960s. The predilection for democratic governance systems was also discernible in the activities of the Pan-African Movement and Congresses, including the landmark 1945 Manchester Conference, which had in attendance many delegates from mainland Africa. The Internet revolution in Africa also contributed significantly to the swing in favour of democracy on the continent. Social Media platforms like Facebook, You Tube, Google, WhatsApp, Blackberry, etc. (18)

According to Sesay the Africans and their intellectuals take the law in their hands to determine the system of government they want. They reject autocracy and establish democracy using the available channels of correspondence including social media platforms such as Twitter, Whatsapp and Google. But if Wanyama's argument is right, why has Somalia, Mali, Nigeria, Uganda, Zimbabwe grappled with military coups? Why has Libya never had a democratic government since 1969? Not all African governments have democratic regimes. Egypt's democratic president Mohammed Mursi was overthrown by the Egyptian army; the Egyptian regime today is military friendly regime. There generally is a flare for autocratic regimes in countries with hot and dry climates or those endowed with natural resources such as gold, uranium and oil; for example, Democratic Republic of Congo, Libya, Egypt, Nigeria, Somalia, South Africa and Arab nations such as Saudi Arabia. Could there be a nexus between ecological factors and the political system chosen by a community?

In Chapter three, I investigate how the ecological environment dictates the political structures of societies in selected works of prose fiction. I will interrogate the role of Mother Nature on the choice of systems of government such as autocracy, democracy, aristocracy and monarchy in contemporary novels. These novels include Mohamed's *Orchard of Lost Soul's*, Safi Abdi's *Offspring of Paradise*, El Saadawi's *God Dies by the Nile* and Matar's *The Return* .The chapter will have at least three sub chapters to give adequate evidence.

3.1 Slavery and Colonialism: Ecological Setting and Growth of Despotism

If there are historical events that nurtured the tradition of dictatorship in our world then they were colonialism and slavery. Although most scholars associate dictatorship with political power, dictatorship involves many other elements in citizens' personal lives. According to Liden (2014), "in dictatorships there are methods other than competitive elections used for distributing political power, and in such societies the political and civil rights of individuals are frequently violated" (53). Liden therefore associates autocracy with any leadership style including at family level in which the rights of individuals are not respected. With the advent of slavery and colonialism, the rights of many Africans were violated by autocratic styles of leaderships on the slave farms and colonies. As the causes of these two historical incidents, many scholars tend to take a homocentric approach without any mention of ecological factors. As much as racism played a role in the hunting and enslavement of African slaves, it is the contention of this subchapter that ecological factors formed the foundation of the rise and development of slavery and colonialism. Angeles L. (2013) observes:

> Sugar production, the single largest employer of slave labour in the Americas, can surely be characterized as effort-intensive. The main tasks involve cutting, chopping, and transporting the cane stalks; followed by a crushing process to extract its juices. The time between cutting and juice extraction must be minimized in order to avoid

> desiccation or fermentation. In tropical countries cane sugar grows almost continually throughout the year so that the labour-intensive process of harvesting and crushing actually takes place year-round (as opposed to what happens in temperate agriculture. (p. 10)

This passage confirms that the ecological conditions of the Americas favoured sugar farming, which prompted many world powers to seek for colonial territories there. Spain, Portugal, France, Great Britain and France conquered territories in Americas and Caribbean to carry out sugarcane farming. The ecological conditions suitable for sugar farming cannot be ignored in the slavery enterprise. According to Verhenye Willy, these ecological conditions include "high temperatures, plenty of sunlight, large quantities of water (at least 1500 mm of rain per year unless grown with irrigation), fertile soils, and good drainage" (p. 2), and they were the perquisite to sugar farming in the Americas and Caribbean. For Angeles, the labour demands for sugarcane compelled the farmers to seek for labour beyond the Americas. At a time when many machines had not been invented, the "cutting, chopping, and transporting the cane stalks; followed by a crushing process to extract its juices" called for availability of suitable labour. Williams (1944) avers that "slavery was not born out of racism: rather racism was a consequence of slavery" (p.7). William suggests that ecological and economic factors conspired to institute slavery and its social and political effects. In her exposition of slavery in the Caribbean, Udofia (2013) asserts:

> The lure of gold, sugar and slaves thus precipitated imperialist forays into the area by Spain, Portugal, Britain,

France and the Netherlands. Each of these imperialists fought to obtain a considerable share of the Caribbean wealth. And this gave rise naturally to piracy, double-crossing, brutality and lack of cohesion among the powers. (p.57)

The raw materials that attracted callous institutions of slavery and colonialism in the Caribbean arise from the crux of Mother Nature. While Mother Earth produced gold in the Caribbean, the ecological conditions favoured the growing of sugar that demanded intense labour for exploitation. The search for cheap labour attracted slave owners to cheap slaves in Africa. There were many slave traders in Africa who raided and sold slaves to Europe cheaply (Angeles, p. 18). Mother Nature therefore played a crucial in the establishment of slavery and its attendant autocratic regime.

Similarly, it is absurd to delink the advent of colonialism from Mother Earth and what she possesses. Although many scholars have cited social factors such as desire to civilise "primitive races" as one cause of colonialism, the major cause of colonial expansion to Africa are associated with material endowments of Africa and Europe. Koponen J. (1993) writes:

> European economy and society underwent a profound transformation during the nineteenth century. The source of this transformation was the unprecedented development of forces and relations of production that is usually referred to as the Industrial Revolution but could more properly be called the breakthrough of industrial capitalism. It led to a

tremendous increase in production and productivity. Having started in the latter half of the eighteenth century in the British cotton industry, industrial capitalism spread at the turn of the century to Belgium and France and then to Germany and the United States. (p.121)

The growth of industrialisation was tied to availability of raw materials such as cotton, water, copper, steel, iron, oil, which were used to produce finished goods to be sold to the colonies. These colonies would also increase supply of raw materials to promote the expansion of the industrial revolution. This is why colonialists were attracted to African nations with best ecological conditions. A British character, Thorne Mackay in Mulwa (2004) comments about the economic importance of African colonies, "[t]urmoil in Africa means a great loss to the empire. Africa supports, nay maintains the Empire" (p.4). The character Thorne singles out the mineral resources and oil as the major pull factor that has sustained British colonization of African nations.

3.2 Slavery and Development of Autocracy: Violation of Human Rights in Slave Narratives and Novels

The foregoing discussion clarifies the concealed role of Mother Nature in establishing slavery and colonialism. Determined to attain industrial and economic supremacy, most Europeans established the institution of slavery that was run with ruthless efficiency. This subsection demonstrates how slavery nurtured dictatorial style of leadership in attempt to maximize productivity of slaves with reference to two slave Narratives: Douglass' *The Narrative of the Life of Frederic Douglass, an American Slave*, Jacob's *Incidents in the life of Slave Girl* and Morrison' *Beloved*. The section investigates how the search for economic progress through sugar farming institutes slavery, an autocratic regime that is later transferred to colonialism.

Douglass' *Narrative of the Life of Frederic Douglass, an American Slave* is a slave narrative that shows the plight of slaves in the United States before the American civil war. Slaves are ruled by a regimented system in which power flows from the slave master, to the overseer, the mistress with slaves occupying the least stave with animals. Douglass raises the curtain to reveal the constant violations of rights of black slaves, which demonstrates the devious nature of autocracy. Commenting on Douglass slave narrative, Brian Warnick (2008), observes that "slavery is not entirely characterized by physical confinement and intimidation; it also arms itself with pedagogical tactics meant to squelch the ability to be free" (1). In other words, the autocratic nature of slavery moves from physical to mental subjugation, which is the focus of this analysis.

Physical subjugation of slaves takes different forms taken by slave masters and overseers in *The Narrative of the life of Frederic Douglass, the American Slave*. When slaves are born, they are separated from their mothers to destroy the child-mother bond. This is a gross violation of the child's right, a denial of parenting. Douglass says, "[m]y mother and I were separated when I was but an infant—before I knew her as my mother. It was a common custom, in the part of Maryland from which I ran away to part children from their mothers at a very early age" (16). The ideas was to effect commodification of the slave, nurture a beastly nature for them to serve the labour demands and adapt to being shoved from region to region. Low a beast of burden, the slave had to be sold, beaten, hired and killed. Humane attachments to parents would hinder such aims. DeNeen Brown (2018) writes:

> A mother unleashed a piercing scream as her baby was ripped from her arms during a slave auction. Even as a lash cut her back, she refused to put her baby down and climb atop an auction block [...]But the child was torn from the arms of its mother amid the most heart-rending shrieks from the mother and child on the one hand, and the bitter oaths and cruel lashes from the tyrants on the other." Her mother was sold to the highest bidder.

The slave master in this passage wants the mother for the market, either to beef up his capital or for culling. Any farmer will always assess their stock of cows to eradicate the infertile, weak, and unproductive ones. The slave master has singled out this female slave for culling to enhance economic productivity of the slave holding. Female slaves, for instance were not allowed to have any love relationships with black slaves. Douglass narrates the story of aunt Hester who was caught by the master, Anthony in the presence of a lover. The punishment was severe: he took her to the kitchen, stripped her to the waist, "leaving her neck, shoulders and back entirely naked" and caned her with a cow skin, warm red blood dripping to the floor" (p. 20). This is the same experience

Linda has in Jacob's *Incidents in the Life of the Slave Girl*. When she finds a fiancé to marry, the master adjures her to desist from such relationships. Linda says, "[m]y master met me at every turn reminding me that I belonged to him, swearing by heaven and earth that he will compel me to submit to him" (31). Dr Flint, Linda's slave master lusts for her so much that he builds a house for her in a distant farm. What is the slave master's interest in the female slave?

In Morrison's *Beloved*, female slaves are forced to have children with their masters as way of increasing the capital base and much needed labour that slave masters needed. The protagonist Sethe is described as "breeder" at Mr Garner's house. The master is exhilarated by Sethe's fertility as her three or four children were being raised to "to take back to Kentucky, raise properly to do the work Sweet Home desperately needed" (p. 184). The master was tremendously excited of her "ten breeding years" (184). The female slave therefore fitted into the industrial capitalism of which base was ecological setting of sugarcane farming and mining. Besides working on the sugarcane plantations, she could reproduce new slaves for the slave owner to sell or apply on the farm. Celia Cussen (2016) et al observes that female slaves were more valuable in urban Santiago than male slaves, most likely a result of female slaves being used as domestic servants (p. 9). As much as domestic work formed one of the major roles of female slaves, Cussen et. al. are incorrect to cite it as the major reason why female slaves were treasured. Morrison contends that female slaves gratified sexual desires of masters and their sons. In case they conceived, the offspring were added to the list slaves to be sold or offer labour.

The female slave Babby Saggs in Morrison's *Beloved was* pressured by the master to have many children to meet the capital and labour demands of the farm. Subsequently, she had eight children with six fathers. The narrator says, "[h]er two girls, neither of whom had their adult teeth were sold and gone and she had not been able to wave good bye" (p. 29). Indeed this is violation of a mother's rights, hence dictatorship as suggested by Liden (2014). There is general tendency to deny female slaves the right to motherhood and they cannot turn to any institution for redress. Baby Suggs decides to bribe the master with sex to save her third child, but "she was traded for lumber and found herself pregnant by the master who had promised not to sell the boy" (29). The masters therefore take advantage of the desperate slave mothers to derive sexual pleasures. Some slaves mate with white masters and their sons in turns. The female slave Ella in Morrison's *Beloved* is locked up in a room to mate two men, slave master and his son. For a full year, Ella remembered every bit of it (p. 146), which is a violation of her individual liberties.

Jacobs explores the same violations of female slaves in the character of Linda. Her decision to maintain purity for marriage is thwarted when the master, Dr Flint violates the marriage vows with his wife to pursue Linda day in day out. Linda has no power to maintain sex morals as held by Christian young women in the south. Linda says of a female slave that if "God has bestowed beauty upon her, it will prove her greatest curse" (p. 31) because the lewd master will seduce her day by day until she loses her purity. Scared of the mistress in the house, Dr Flint threatens to kill those female slaves he has had sex with if they reveal the affairs. Linda says:

> Other female slaves knew too well the guilty practices under that roof and they were aware that to speak of them was an offense that never went unpunished [...] Dr Flint swore he would kill me if I was not as silent as a grave. (32)

In slave holdings, such threats as Dr Flints' were not wanton; the spite with which a slave was held accentuated cruelty so much that most female slaves would be killed like insects by both masters and mistresses. One thing Jacobs underscores is how the dictatorial regime under which the female slave lives denies her the right to a sound sex life because of the ecological background that has placed severe labour demands on her sex. Just as cow that should meet the owner's capital demands, the female salve has to have sex with Master, his son; and whoever the master desires to beget more slaves. Jacobs writes:

> How had those years dealt with her slave sister, the little playmate of her childhood? She, also, was very beautiful; but the flowers and sunshine of love were not for her. She drank the cup of sin, and shame, and misery, whereof her persecuted race are compelled to drink. (p.33)

To exploit the Natural resources, the capitalistic system that Koponen refers to in the introduction the female slave occupies the pivotal role of reproducing the workers through sex. The workers are the black people; the system believes are the hands that can do the "cutting, chopping, and transporting the cane stalks; followed by a crushing process to extract its juices" (Angele, p.10). Black bodies were viewed as the most suitable part of the labour machine for the exploitation of Natural resources, (Cussen et. al., p. 9). A regimented system had to be established to facilitate their efficient participation in Mother Nature's exploitation. Right from the kitchen, slaves had to be productive and loyal. When Mrs Hick in *The Narrative of the Life of Frederic Douglass* gives a female slave a baby to look after, but she starts dozing for missing sleep few days before, the mistress does not waste her time on advice. The slave is in America to exploit Mother Nature for profits: not dozing around. Subsequently, she just "seized an oak stick of wood by the fire place and with it broke the girl's nose and breastbone" (p. 36-37). It is tragic how the young female slave is startled from sleep by a death blow. Frederic describes the blow as "mangling her person in the most horrible manner [...] so that the girl expired in a few hour afterward" (p. 36). For Mrs Hick's, by dozing to neglect the baby, the female slave had relegated her role as stipulated by the ecological environment. This is why Linda fears when Dr Flint threatens to kill her if she reveals his lewdness to the mistress. It is her role in this ecosystem to reproduce slaves for labour force. Babby Suggs in Morrison's *Beloved* appraises her Master as quite benevolent because he does not force her to have sex with her sons. She says Mr Garner is noble because he does not "bring her sons to her cabin with orders to lay with her like they did in Carolina" (p. 173). This is a dictatorship that transgresses all moral bounds to elevate moral decadence.

The slave masters in *The Narrative of the Life of Frederic Douglass, the American Slave* execute the autocratic script with shocking exactness. Mr Bead Bondly, for instance detests the propensity of Colonel Lloyd's slaves to fish Oysters near his farm. Infuriated, Mr Bondly does not care to warn them of trespass; he "picked his musket, came down the shore and blew its deadly contents on the poor slave" (p.37). Although a homocentric critique will focus on the racial othering of slaves, the autocracy in this episode is aimed at controlling Mother Nature's endowments: the Oysters near Bondly's farm, which he considers worthier than the neighbour's slaves who do not work for him.

The story of Mr Gore, an overseer with the slave Demby demonstrates the pinnacle of autocracy of slavery. Douglass describe the overseer as "artful, cruel obdurate" (34). Throughout his dealings, Gore "spoke but to command, and he commanded but to be obeyed" (p.33). These autocratic tendencies should be considered in the immediate context of coercing slaves to offer labour in sugar plantations and gold mines. The system is regimented and mechanized to compel slaves to exploit natural resources. Mr Gore was known to use few words and would only order a slave to go where he was supposed to go two times, and shoot the third time. This day, in the presence of Douglass, he ordered the male slave Demby to go where he was. When he refused, Douglass and fellow slaves waited for the third call. It did not come, instead Gore "raised his musket to his face, taking a deadly aim at his standing victim and in an instant poor Demby was no more. His mangled body sank out of sight and blood and brains marked the water where he had stood" (p. 35). Similarly, Jacobs in *Incidents in the Life of a Slave Girl* shows how a Planter called Mr Litch used crude punishments to punish slaves that destabilized peace on the sugar plantation. He would tie a rope around a man's body and suspend him from the ground. A fire would be kindled over the man from which would be suspended is pieces of fat pork. As it cooked, the scalding drops of fat continually fell on the bare flesh of the victim (p. 51). In one shocking event, some slaves stole his meat and wine and Jacobs reports:

> No words were used, but a club felled them to the ground. A rough box was their coffin, and their interment was a dog's burial. Nothing was said. Murder was so common on his plantation that he feared to be alone after nightfall. He might have believed in ghosts. (p. 51-52)

Although from the face value Mr Litch appears to protect his wine, the real aim is to protect his sugar, mineral and other crops on the farm. In fact, Jacobs underscores his dependency on Mother Nature when she describes Litch as a man of little education, "an ill-bred, uneducated man, but very wealthy" (p. 51). Many of these slave masters have gained wealth by sheer exploitation Mother Nature's endowments rather than homocentric pursuits such as formal education. In the attempt to control what Nature has given them, slave Masters become dictatorial and warlike. Litch therefore employs overseers and pays them well and beyond that [t]here was a jail and a whipping post on his grounds; and whatever cruelties were perpetrated there, they passed without comment" (51). For example a male slave who resisted being whipped would be left at the mercy of hounds that would tear his flesh from bones (p.55).

This is the same situation found in Morrison's Beloved when male slaves such as Paul D are chained on the way to Georgia, and are not allowed to ask for meals:

"Want some breakfast, nigger?"

"Yes sir."

"Hungry, Nigger?"

"Here you go." (p.132)

They are shot dead for asking for meals. Autocracy is therefore a style of leadership that arises out the desire to control natural resources and manipulate the forces of production. The constant regimentation has a hidden hand of the ecological environment as humankind struggles to exploit Mother Nature for their material benefit.

3.3 Colonialism and Rise of Dictatorship: Violation of Human Rights in Contemporary Novels

These human rights violations are extended to colonized citizens during colonialism particularly in the Caribbean and Africa. Out of the need to exploit the natural resources, colonialists introduce direct rule in countries with enormous resources and indirect rule in regions without resources. In South Africa, for instance, the presence of enormous resources prompted the Boers to introduce the cruellest system of colonialism that takes centuries in which the black people are oppressed. This subsection will focus on the role of ecological factors in development of autocratic colonial system of government with reference to Alex La Guma's *In the Fog of a Season's End* and Ngugi wa Thiong'o's *A Grain of Wheat*. The choice of the two primary texts is justified because they are set in South Africa and Kenya respectively during the colonial period. The two states, South Africa and Kenya have ecological conditions that favour crop farming and are endowed with mineral resources that attracted the colonialism.

Alex la Guma's *In the Fog of a Season's End* is the story of Beaukes and Tekwane who run an underground movement to fight for independence in South Africa. Beaukes has to dodge police surveillance as he moves from one part of the country to another to bolster networks among freedom fighters in attempt to dislodge the autocratic apartheid regime. His colleague, Elias Tekwane, the undisputable leader of the movement is apprehended and tortured to death. La Guma uses macabre tone to show the atrocities committed by the autocratic regime, but expresses hope that the excesses are the last symptoms of the end of the regime. Ngugi's *A Grain of Wheat* is a historical novel that dwells on the sacrifices that Kenyans made in the struggle against colonial oppression. Ngugi shows the plight of freedom fighters in their determination to liberate their land from invaders who enslaved Kenyans for seven decades. Men who join the struggle are detained, tortured, and even killed by public hanging to serve as lessons to the public. One amazing thing is the realization that in spite of the colonial pretences, the colonialist comes to Kenya to alienate land from African peoples.

Although colonial exploitation in Africa has been highly politicized, a critical examination of its causes had great ecological influences. Most Europeans were attracted by the favourable ecological conditions in Africa. The history of the migration of the Dutch to South Africa confirms how Mother Nature played an essential role in the colonisation of the nation. Oliver (2017) writes, "[w]hereas it was seemingly the intention of the Dutch to only establish a halfway station at the Cape, Van Riebeeck soon realised that the land had immense possibilities and only a year after they had landed in the Cape, he released nine Company servants to start full-time farming to the eastern side of Table Mountain" (p.4). Throughout apartheid regime, Van Riebeeck is singled out as the first man to arrive in South Africa to lay claim to African land because of its fertility and abundance of mineral resources. Lord Churchill (1897), confirms that the Boers loves the Agricultural land in South Africa:

> The Boer farmer personifies useless idleness. Occupying a farm of from six thousand to ten thousand acres, he contents himself with raising a herd of a few hundred head of cattle, which are left almost entirely to the care of the natives whom he employs. It may be asserted, generally with truth, that he never plants a tree, never digs a well, never makes a road, never grows a blade of corn ... .He passes his day doing absolutely nothing beyond smoking and drinking coffee. He is perfectly uneducated. With the exception of the Bible, every word of which in its most

literal interpretation he believes with fanatical credulity, he never opens a book, he never even reads a newspaper. His simple ignorance is unfathomable, and this in stolid composure he shares with his wife, his sons, his daughters, being proud that his children should grow up as ignorant, as uncultivated, as hopelessly unprogressive as himself. In the winter time he moves with his herd of cattle into the better pastures and milder climate of the low country veldt, and lives as idly and uselessly in his waggon as he does in his farmhouse. The summer sees him returning home, and so on [sic], year after year, generation after generation, the Boer farmer drags out the most ignoble existence ever experienced by a race with any pretensions to civilization. (94–95)

In this passage that infuriated the Dutch after the book's publication, Lord Churchill confirms how the Boers had no other interests in South Africa besides its land and ecological conditions favourable for farming. Their spite for education shows how they are solely concerned about the Mother Nature's impact on their lives. The use the word "unprogressive" and "uncultivated" further elevates their dependency on Mother Nature rather than scientific knowledge that the British are interested in. Winter and summer, aspects of the Natural environment dictate their migratory patterns from year to year. Their unwillingness to plant trees, build roads and dig wells suggests that the Boers are content with the ecological conditions of South Africa. Wyk Smith (2003) observes that Churchill's ideas causes outrage among Dutch speaking people and laid the foundation to the Anglo-Boer War of 1899-1902 (p. 429) over the lucrative natural resources of South Africa. This war between the two foreign powers over South Africa paved way for dictatorial colonial regimes in South Africa. This was the case after the National party won the elections in 1948. Oliver and Oliver (2017) describe the most dictatorial rule in South Africa (p.5). Indeed out of the desire to control the natural resources, La Guma demonstrates how the apartheid regime developed autocratic tendencies in South Africa in *In the Fog of Season's End*.

As the novel begins, the writer confirms what Churchill refers to as "uneducated" (94-97) aspects of the Boers through the manner in which they handle Elias Tekwane, the freedom fighter. The Boer solders choose vulgar and colloquial dialects and behave contrary to what is expected of a race on a mission to "civilise" the Africans. After Tekwane gives a short speech to remind them about their propensity to shoot black people, one soldier says, "[s]hit, you are not at a bloody public meeting" (p. 6). It is ironical that Boers who hold themselves so highly as epitome of culture, should choose words such as "shit" and swear words such as "bloody" to address the so called "uncivilised person" by virtue of his inferior race. The soldier goes on, "[w]e will make you piss blood you baboon" (p.6). The reader is again shocked by the 'civilised' man's use the word "piss". Indeed as Churchill contends, besides the desire to protect and exploit land and mineral resources, the Boers have no other interests that would promote their wellbeing and that of Africans.

In Tekwane's words, it is apparent that the apartheid regime, in the its determination to maintain a firm hold on South Africa's natural resources, has consistently maimed and murdered innocent South Africans. Through dozens of oppressive laws, they have otherized black people and treated them like suspects. Some of the major Acts of parliament are related to natural resources. Penelope A. (1987) says that the land Acts of 1913 and 1936, the bulk of the country's land-86.5 percent--has been reserved for whites. Only 13.5 percent of the land can be owned by blacks" (2). The laws are executed ruthlessly by the help of the callous police force and army. Tekwane tells the soldiers:

> You are going to torture me, maybe kill me. But that is the only way you and your people can rule us. You shoot and kill and torture because you cannot rule in any other way a people who reject you. You are reaching the end of the road and going downhill towards a great darkness, so you must take a lot of people with you, because you are selfish and greedy and afraid of the coming darkness. (p. 6)

Tekwane confirms that the apartheid regime does not lead, but "rule" the black people to maintain a monopoly over natural resources. The opposition by black people is a viable threat because they are the majority yet as Penelope elucidates own just 13 percent of the land. They shoot to kill blacks to thwart any threats to the resources. This is the selfishness and greed because the Boers refuse to share natural resources availed by Mother Nature. Similarly, the leader of the liberation Movement in Ngugi's *A Grain of Wheat* avers that the Bristish colonialist have created a police state to rule and control Kenya's natural resources. Pointing at Mahee police statation, he says "[d]estroy that and the Whiteman is gone. He rules with the gun, the lives all black people of Kenya"

(p. 50). Violence therefore takes the form of physical torture and murder. Tekwane is tortured mercilessly because he is the leader of the movement that threatens to take natural resources away from the dominant whites:

> The two security men let the prisoner go and the young man kicked him so that he rolled down and down over the steps, crying out, the handcuffs preventing him from breaking his fall. He lay groaning at the bottom of the steps. The sportsman [...] unzipped his fly and urinated off the steps into the prisoner's face [...] the detectives removed their jackets and the sportsman hit him in the stomach and began to batter him mercilessly with his fists. It was like working at a bag in the gymnasium. When one was tired, the other took over. The prisoner fought for breath and struggled to avoid the blows. (p. 6-7)

Tekwane's torture demonstrates not only the cruelty of the apartheid dictatorship, but the uneducated attribute of Boers. The Sportsman's decision to unzip and "urinated into the prisoner's face" is a clear illustration of what Churchill refers to as the administration's "uncultivation." The detention without trial is another feature lacking in the civilised West from where the Boers hail. Tekwane is declared guilty as charged before being arraigned in any court. The beating is so severe; Tekwane is compared to a sand bag in a gymnasium even as he struggles with his breath. La Guma uses Tekwane's torture and death to represent the plight of African freedom fighters when they are arrested by the dictatorial regime. The same way, British colonialists arrest Kihika, the leader of the liberation movement and torture him callously. Ngugi says "[s]ome say a neck of a bottle was wedged into his body through the anus. Kihika was hanged in public pone Sunday at Rungei market (p. 8). The public hanging is meant to serve as a warning to other Africans. All this use of force arises from the fact that Kihika led Africans to fight for land. In the character Kihika, Ngugi is very clear about the major causes of the advent of colonialism. Kihika tells his friends:

> We went to the church. Mubia in white robes opened the Bible. He said, let us kneel and pray. We knelt down. Mubia said: let us shut our eyes. We did. You know, his remained open so that he could read the word. When we opened our eyes, our land was gone and the sword of flames stood on guard. As for Mubia, he went on reading the word, beseeching us to lay our treasures in heaven where no moth would corrupt them. But he laid his on earth, our earth. (p.7)

Ngugi rejects all other colonialist pretences as reasons for coming to Africa for instance to spread Christianity or civilize the African peoples. Ngugi reiterates Oliver and Oliver's argument that the endowments that Mother Nature ascribed Africa are the major reasons for the coming of Europeans. While the missionary in the above passage preaches the spiritual kingdom, his colleagues are busy scouting for land and in a short while, the Agikuyu land is alienated. "The sword of flames" represents the dictatorial system that is established to guard the resources. This "dictatorial system" that was introduced in Kenya highlands was called direct rule as opposed to indirect rule. It was executed through a number of laws that were passed. Karari Peter (2018) writes:

> The British colonial authorities in Kenya had to find a way to legalize land control, as it had no rights over natives' land. The colonial authorities, therefore, enacted a series of Crown land ordinances to formalize the dispossession of the natives' land. These ordinances led to the appropriation of millions of acres of land that became white highlands. (p. 1)

Like South Africa, direct rule in Kenya was only used in areas with enormous natural resources to enable the colonialists to have full control for exploitation. The African people were therefore exposed to forced labour, denied freedom to move into cities and directed mostly into white settler farms for wage labour. The introduction of hut and poll taxes compelled most Africans to migrate to settler farms to survive. In La Guma's *In the Fog of a Season's End,* Tekwane's father is forced to work in a mine, but what befalls him shows the squalid conditions of his fellow miners. Young Tekwane had come to learn that "his father was killed in a mining accident near Johannesburg, he was buried hundreds of feet below the ground, deeper than any of his ancestors had been buried" (p. 73). The racist dictatorial regime segregated Africans during the payment of compensations because they do not consider Africans, workers. While Tekwane's mother is given two pounds a month, the widows of white miners are paid fifteen pounds a month (p.74). Tekwane later comes to learn that according to the law, blacks are servants rather than workers (133) and therefore their strikes are illegal. Worse still is the condition of the African miners; whereas the whites give animals insurance health covers, their black workers are exposed to toxic substances in the mines without any health insurance cover. Tekwane meets an African miner suffering from phthisis or pulmonary tuberculosis. He is described as "thin and bent and coughed all the time" (132) with an employer that has relieved him his duties to return home without even sweets for his children.

This is the attitude that Dr Lynd portrays towards that African workers at Githima in *A Grain of Wheat*. She values her dog more than African peoples she works with. Her boss John Thompson is worried by her decision to release the dog among African workers without any qualms about the harm it might cause. When the workers throw stones to defend themselves, she begrudges them. She tells Karanja that she detests his previous action of throwing stones at the dog and when he denies, she accuses all Africans as liars. She quips, "[t]he way you people lie?" (p. 18). The belief that Africans are liars has been concocted by the dictatorial regimes to justify their othering to punish and continue controlling their resources. The white characters in Ngugi's *A Grain of Wheat* admit that they love the ecological attributes of Kenya. When Thompson reaches Kenya, he writes to his wife Margery, "I am delighted to touch the red earth of Kenya. I was here during the war and I liked the climate" (34). The words "red earth" and "climate" demonstrate the essential role of ecological factors in the colonial enterprise. The hatred Thompson has for the African people arises from the fact that they are legitimate owners of this beautiful country. In his private journal, he writes:

> Nyeri is full of mountains, hills and deep valleys covered with impenetrable forests. These primordial trees have always awed primitive minds. The darkness and mystery of

the forest have led him (the primitive man) to magic ritual. (P.22)

This extract from Thompson shows the much he loves the land and natural resources of Kenya. It is country endowed with fertile land, forests and has the potential to have minerals resources if explored. But he distastes the aborigines and calls them names: "primitive man" who loves magic. It is quite untrue to argue that the "trees have awed" the Africans because this has been their motherland and they are used to the trees. If there is someone to be awed by Nyeri then it is Thompson.

As a result of his hatred for Africans, Thompson has not just adopted dictatorial racist philosophies, but maintains a mean attitude that has sometimes resulted in massacre of Africans. Besides believing that an African is a liar, Thompson cites Albert Schwelzer, "[t]he Negro is a child and with children, nothing can be done without the use of authority. I have worked in Nyeri, Githima, Kisumu, Ngong. I agree." (p. 23). He therefore does not hide his violence in the presence of Africans. When Mugo visits him to reveal that he knows where Kihika can be found, Thompson spits on his face. In his opinion, "the African is a born actor, that is why he finds it easy to lie" (p. 24). Even when detainees go on a hunger strike at Rira Detention Camp, he orders them to be tortured because in his opinion, they are Africans and hence mere actors. Eleven detainees died (p.19) and his cruelty formed a major discussion in the British House of Commons. The Governor demoted him; he was sent to Githima, as the administrative secretary.

These racist autocratic attitudes are also exhibited in white administrators in La Guma's *In the Fog of a Season's End*. While enrolling for a pass, they assign Tekwane a false age saying, "[h]e is a skelm, a cheat. They are all liars, these. He is too big for seventeen" (p. 126). Like Thompson, they force Tekwane to lower his trousers, confirm whether he is circumcised and declare him twenty years of age. As an African he is both a liar and ignorant and so everything (including age, name, home, job, life) is decided for him. Tekwane would sometimes witness mass eviction of people from white areas to drier parts of the country. He says:

> The police would surround an area, 'a Black spot' in a white zone and load everybody onto a convoy of trucks. Hours later they would arrive in a place the Government had marked out for them on the map and there they would be unloaded: the battered furniture, hastily packed suitcases and boxes, the children wailing in the open veld. (p.130)

This passage shows how the colonialists are determined to reserve for themselves the most ecologically favourable regions of South Africa. Africans are evicted and taken to drier and less productive regions of the country. The last clause, "the children wailing in the open veld" is a standing illustration of the worthlessness of the land in which they have been evicted to. Any protests against such government policies is met with violent action, for example when the African people protest against passes at Sharpeville, the police crash it violently. La Guma says, "[t]he crowd was already bursting away, scattering wide, a jumbled, falling, headlong rush away from the smoking iron muzzles of the guns [...] with the volley came a silence of finality "(p. 104). Many innocent Africans were shot and died in the cold blood because of the racist colonial attitudes as exhibited by Thompson in *A Grain of Wheat*. Similarly, the Boers believe Africans are actors, liars and children; force must be used to achieve anything. As liars, their protest is null and void and this is why many African people are shot. La Guma competes the description of Sharpeville massacre:

> While the living wandered, some aimlessly and others with purpose, among the dead and dying and wounded, the sky muttered darkly at last and started to shed heavy drops of rain. Thunder clashed along the horizon like a duel of artillery and then the rain began to fall steadily to mingle with the blood. (p. 105)

The massacre was so severe that blood flooded on the street; the rain falls to cleanse South Africa of the evil of dictatorship that colonialism has so well sowed. That an innocent people would be shot in the cold blood for asking for their rights, it proves beyond reasonable doubt that colonialism established dictatorship in African nations.

Conclusion

From the foregoing discussion, colonialism was motivated by ecological factors of the colonized territories. It is apparent that where the territory had fertile land and mineral resources such as gold, there was direct rule which meant a more intense form of dictatorship to control those resources. South Africa has severer form of autocracy than Kenya because of availability of abundant mineral resources such as gold. The fertile land around Mount

Kenya necessitated the introduction of direct rule, which caused a lot of suffering in the region. Autocracy is therefore influenced by ecological factors of the region in which people lives.

3.4 The Industrial Revolution and Autocratic Parenting: Mother Nature and Facts in Dicken's *Hard Times*

> The novels dealing with the condition-of-England as a theme are expected to depict contemporary reality in an attempt to reflect the situation of the country at a time of dramatic changes. Dickens reflects the society in a fictional industrial town, describing the differences between the workers (represented in the novel by Stephen Blackpool and Rachael, for they are the only workers Dickens allows to take part in the novel) and the owners of the factories, naming the characters differently from the real persons that influenced the author for their creation.
>
> Miguelinaze (2015, p. 12)

As much as fiction is considered imaginary, some of Dicken's works of fiction are representations of the reality of England in the 19th century. Miguelanaze avers that Dicken's *Hard Times* "reflects" the situation of the industrialisation in England at the time. Miguelinaze observes that the novel demonstrates the actual realities with regards to disputes between industrial owners and workers. This subchapter extends Miguelinaze's argument to ecological factors that contributed to industrialisation in Dicken's England, which most critics ignore. The subsection investigates the role of Mother Nature in influencing the industrialisation in England with reference to Dicken's *Hard Times*. In other words, did the ecological endowments of Britain contribute to the industrial revolution or everything should be pegged on homocentric factors?

Scholars suggest that besides human factors, industrialisation in England was influenced by ecological factors. Clark G. (2005) writes:

> By 1850, at the apogee of its power, Britain had 1.8% of world population. The area of the British Isles is only about 0.16% of the world land mass. Yet Britain then produced two-thirds of world output of coal and one half of world production of cotton textiles and iron. Output per worker was higher in Britain than in any other country. (1)

Clark argues that England was endowed with raw materials such as Iron, coal and cotton which inspired the English to embark on their exploitation. The availability of coal, cotton and iron was in such an amazing quantities that Britain contributed two thirds and half of the world production respectively. It is apparent that Britain had the ecological conditions conducive for cotton production. Constable G. A (1988) observes that coffee requires hot and dry conditions to growth and temperature during growing season as a great influence on the crop" (1). Being a novel dealing with the "condition of England" *Hard Times* captures these realities in the 19th century, sometimes mentioning the raw materials that Clark (2005) refers to.

> Time went on in Coketown like its own machinery: so much material wrought up, so much fuel consumed, so many powers worn out, so much money made. But, less inexorable than iron, steel, and brass, it brought its varying seasons even into that wilderness of smoke and brick, and made the only stand that ever was made in the place against its direful uniformity. (99)

Dickens' Coke Town represents industrial towns in England such as Norwich and Worcester in the 19th century England (Clark, p. 8). The industries in these cities persistently turn raw materials into finished goods. The statement "so much raw material wrought up" suggests that the industry pulverizes the available raw materials: iron, cotton, steel into finished goods. The "so much fuel consumed" is the coal, which Clark refers to as one of the major raw materials England was endowed with at the time. The smoke is a product of burning of coal that England is very much in possession of. According to the Greenpeace (2005):

> The environmental effects of coal use range from the poisoning of local rivers by acid mine drainage to the global problem of climate change caused by CO2 (carbon dioxide) emissions. 'Clean coal' technologies are expensive and are still unable to completely remove harmful emissions from coal-fired power plants. (p. 1)

The above effects are clearly evident in Dicken's *Hard Times* because of the availability of coal in the English ecosystem. Whereas Greenpeace emphasizes the effect of coals to the Natural environment, this subchapter underscores the availability of coal in the ecological environment as a prerequisite to its exploitation. The English characters in Dickens' *Hard Times* are compelled by availability of coal, iron and cotton to exploit coal for their industrialisation in Coketown. Of Coke Town Dickens writes:

> It was a town of red brick, or of brick that would have been red if the smoke and ashes had allowed it; but as matters stood, it was a town of unnatural red and black like the painted face of a savage. It was a town of machinery and tall chimneys, out of which interminable serpents of smoke trailed themselves for ever and ever, and never got uncoiled. It had a black canal in it, and a river that ran purple with ill-smelling dye, and vast piles of building full of windows where there was a rattling and a trembling all day long, and where the piston of the steam-engine worked monotonously up and down, like the head of an elephant in a state of melancholy madness. (p .25)

In this passage, coal as a pollutant is evident in this as the smoke forms serpents of smoke in the sky. The river has also been polluted by industrial waste such that it resembles "ill-smelling dye"; which confirms Clark's mention of iron and steel industries. The red bricks are not red because of air pollution; the houses in Coketown have turned from brick red to "black like the painted face of the savage". The availability of coal in Coketown has not just fuelled industrialisation but also affected every aspect of life in Coketown.

The industrial revolution, for instance, elevates a utilitarian philosophy and mechanization that spills into the education system. The teachers, industrial owners and parents adopt a dictatorial regime that does not allow discussion at any point in life. Dickens portrays Josiah Bounderby and Thomas Gradgrind as rigid and autocratic because of the desire to use science to exploit the natural resources in Coketown. Bounderby is a manufacturer, who is described as:

> A man with a great puffed head and forehead, swelled veins in his temples, and such a strained skin to his face that it seemed to hold his eyes open, and lift his eyebrows up. A man with a pervading appearance on him of being inflated like a balloon, and ready to start. A man who could never sufficiently vaunt himself a self-made man. A man who was always proclaiming, through that brassy speaking-trumpet of a voice of his, his old ignorance and his old poverty. A man who was the Bully of humility. (p.18)

Mr Bounderby's belief in the use of science to exploit ecological resources affects his character such that he becomes very autocratic. His character brings into focus Bacon's assessment of the indoctrinating attributes of science. According to Bacon, "[t]hose who have handled sciences have been either men of experiment or men of dogmas…" (XCV). Bounderby with his friend, Gradgrind indeed are men of "experiment and dogma".

They have elevated the tenets of enlightenment into an unquestionable belief that those under them cannot question. The concept of "self-made man" that Bounderby harps on represents the enlightenment propensity to reject religion and its resolve to master her destiny. As a result of this embrace for the novelty, Bounderby discounts the role of his parents in his present success. When Stephen Black Pool asks him advice on how he can divorce his wife, Bounderby takes him through the dozen restrictions and conventions of modernism that have been installed to oppress the poor citizens. As to whether there is any other way Stephen can use, Bounderby says, "certainly not" (p.81), in support of a legal system which only accesses justice to the moneyed classes. Stephen expresses the oppressive attribute of the mechanized system by saying, "tis a muddle. 'Tis just a muddle a' toogether, an' the sooner I am dead, the better" (p. 82). Just like there exists a logical process of extracting natural resources in Bounderby's world, he endorses a logical process of solving disputes. He reprimands Black Pool:

> Don't you talk nonsense, my good fellow,' said Mr. Bounderby, 'about things you don't understand; and don't you call the Institutions of your country a muddle, or you'll get yourself into a real muddle one of these fine mornings. The institutions of your country are not your piecework, and the only thing you have got to do, is, to mind your piece-work. You didn't take your wife for fast and for loose; but for better for worse. If she has turned out worse - why, all we have got to say is, she might have turned out better.' (p. 83)

The reference to institutions is a modernist element of modernist state that underscores the impact of science on the political organisation of England. Many rules are established to curtail the freedom of citizens, most of which require greater financial responsibility to find justice. The state encouraged sycophancy and paranoia and takes away the rights of the people; hence weakening rather than empowering them. Bounderby compels Black Pool to be subservient to a system that denies him freedom by legislating on morality. He is shocked that he cannot leave the relationship he willingly started because of so many legal hurdles placed in his way. These are the dogma, Bacon associated with "man of science" since so many rules, though made by man cannot be unmade until Black Pool goes to the House of Commons and Court with a lot of money, he cannot find.

Grandgrind turns the school into an oppressive dogmatic institution because for him it is an industry that churns students into finished products such as steel and textile material. Given the pertinence of science in the extraction and processing of raw materials into finished goods, Gradgrind adopts it in every aspect of life and therefore the ecological environment moulds him into the kind of teacher he becomes. Knowledge for Gradgrind is that which can be utilised in the industrial development of Coketown. Anything other than this does not fit the threshold of knowledge. In the first chapter, "The One Thing Needful", Gradgrind is introduced as follows:

> 'Now, what I want is, Facts. Teach these boys and girls nothing but Facts. Facts alone are wanted in life. Plant

nothing else, and root out everything else. You can only form the minds of reasoning animals upon Facts: nothing else will ever be of any service to them. This is the principle on which I bring up my own children, and this is the principle on which I bring up these children. Stick to Facts, sir!' (p.3)

Gradgrind makes this speech to the new teacher Mr Chokumchild in front of all the children to underscore the kind of education the new teacher has to inculcate in the young minds. Opinions and fancies are forbidden; the teacher has to focus on that is scientifically proven to be utilised in the industrial development of Coketown. The teaching of literature, for instance, will not contribute to the extraction and manufacture of iron, steel and textile and hence of little use to the economic health of Coketown. Zubair A. (2016) avers that Gradgrind lays "a lot of emphasis on the one-sidedness of his utilitarian educational philosophy and was helped by the square wall of his forehead, by his mouth, which was wide, thin and stiff, by his voice, which was rigid, dry and dictatorial" (6). For Zubair, an education system of which focus is desire to meet the demands of the ecological environment encourages rigidity and dictatorship. All the children are forced to adhere to the dogmatic rules of science even in simple definitions of names of animals. All other fields of knowledge such as religion and the arts are shoved aside and any children with such tendencies severely criticized. Knowledge has to be either mathematics, biological science or physical sciences because the natural resources in Coketown (coal, steel, iron) dictate so. Gradgrind symbolizes this utilitarian philosophy as quoted below:

Thomas Gradgrind, sir. A man of realities. A man of facts and calculations. A man who proceeds upon the principle that two and two are four, and nothing over, and who is not to be talked into allowing for anything over. Thomas Gradgrind, sir - peremptorily Thomas - Thomas Gradgrind. With a rule and a pair of scales, and the multiplication table always in his pocket, sir, ready to weigh and measure any parcel of human nature, and tell you exactly what it comes to. It is a mere question of figures, a case of simple arithmetic. (p. 4)

The use of "sir" in the passage signifies the dictatorial aspects of the dogmatic education system that compels learners to master scientific conventions regardless of their taste for the arts. The rules have to be obeyed to acquire the knowledge they will need to extract and process the natural resources of Coketown. Maths is instrumental in calculation of weights of chemicals needed in the production of finished goods in the factories. Chemical and civil engineers rather than comedians and singers will be required in the steel and textile industries in Coketown. As a teacher poised to support the industrialisation programme of Coketown, Gradgrind is so adapt in scientific principles that he walks around with multiplication tables in his pocket. He wants all his students to become scientists and reprimands those who stray from it as they would sabotage the industrialisation that Mother Nature requires to exploit the available resources. Dickens suggests that the children were beaten into submission to acquire the scientific knowledge required for industrialisation in England. In one of the magazines, Dickens (cited from introduction of Hard Times) wrote:

I saw a Minister of State, sitting in his closet; and round about him, rising from the country which he governed, up to the Eternal Heavens, was a low dull Howl of Ignorance... I saw 30,000 children hunted, flogged, imprisoned, but not taught, all joined in this cry. . . . The Minister said, Hearken to this cry. What shall we do to stay (stop) it?' But in the end, the Minister shrugged his shoulder and replied, it is a great wrong, but it will last many a time.' (10)

The children are therefore forced to memorise facts to hasten the acquisition of the physical sciences to be utilised in exploitation of the resources in the ecological environment. This is the dictatorial style of administration in schools manifested through children being "hunted, flogged and imprisoned" but their cry is not heeded. In spite of the anguish these children go through, the minister can only say "it is a great wrong, but it will last many a time". The government is therefore helpless in the face of the evil being propagated by the education system because the ecological endowments of England dictate what kind of education the children should have. There is no doubt that that characters such as Josiah Bounderby have entertained gluttony that has drawn them to elevate science to exploit the available natural resources for material gains.

As a result of the tendency to adhere to utilitarian philosophy, the children are barred from living normal life; in fact general nouns for animals are replaced by scientific terms. It is also confounding to see teachers disapproving any leaning towards the arts. Pupils are not allowed to imagine, joke or develop their emotions. In the chapter, "Murdering the Innocents" Thomas Gradgrind reprimands Sissy for using the pet name that her father gave her. Pet names transgress the seriousness of facts that the school inculcates in learners. Gradgrind observes, "Sissy is not a name [...] 'Don't call yourself Sissy. Call yourself Cecilia." (p.5). it is ironical that the teacher does not use names to refer to them; he uses numbers to exhibit his passion for Maths and Science. Sissy is therefore "Girl number twenty" who offends him further when she asserts that her father practices horse riding. Such entertaining games run counter to the philosophy of science that Gradgrind detests. He warns Sissy, "[y]ou mustn't tell us about the ring, here. Very well, then. Describe your father as a horsebreaker. He doctors sick horses, I dare say?" Sissy is being forced to assign her father a different profession that is relevant to the scientific community of Coketown. Horse riding is irrelevant to the exploitation of iron, cotton and Coal; children are compelled to refrain from it. To underscore the scientific attributes of the age, a horse cannot be defined in lay person's language. The children have to use scientific jargon or be punished. Bitzer gives facts about the horse:

> Quadruped. Graminivorous. Forty teeth, namely twenty-four grinders, four eye-teeth, and twelve incisive. Sheds coat in the spring; in marshy countries, sheds hoofs, too. Hoofs hard, but requiring to be shod with iron. Age known by marks in mouth. (6)

The teacher compliments Bitzer for teaching Girl number twenty these facts about a horse. It is a positive sign in the utilitarian direction because when Bitzer he will either become a veterinary doctor to treat animals or a medical doctor to treat cases that take illness from the polluted ecological environment. Similarly, Sissy's assertion that she can place in her room a carpet with "representations of flowers" because she fancies flowers annoys her teachers. They adjure never to fancy:

> "Ay, ay, ay! But you mustn't fancy,' cried the gentleman, quite elated by coming so happily to his point. 'That's it! You are never to fancy."
>
> "You are not, Cecilia Jupe,' Thomas Gradgrind solemnly repeated, 'to do anything of that kind." (p.8)

Scientific facts stipulate that a horse and a flower, cannot exist on a carpet; Sissy's propensity to place them there exhibits her vivid imagination, which she is forbidden to explore. The faculty of imagination is inconsistent to the industrial demands of Coketown to exploit the available natural resources. Sissy has to be compelled to shed all attributes of imagination and adopt facts, partly because of the dictates of Mother Nature. Indeed characters that have aligned their aspirations to the demands of the ecological environment, for example, Bounderby, are wealthy, but those that have taken to careers that elevate imagination are poor.

From the foregoing discussion, it is apparent that Mother Nature has instituted dictatorial style of leadership in school and family. The presence of cotton, coal, iron influence the industrial revolution in Coketown, which determines the education system and style of administration. The teachers adopt a highhanded style of administration to inculcate their philosophy of facts among learners. The industrial owners employ authoritarian tactics in the handling of workers such as Stephen Black pool. The modernist ideals of high culture introduce dogmatic conventions that oppress the poor whenever they seek justice. Blackpool refers to these as "muddle" since he feels oppressed by the modern system of government, which only favours the rich.

3.5. Mother Nature and the Council of Elders: Consensus and Democracy in Contemporary Novels

Many African communities were ruled by a council of elders who made decisions through discussion before a consensus was reached when the majority supported it. In the previous sub chapters, it was apparent that dictatorship thrived in regions endowed with valuable minerals such as coal, iron and gold. In the contemporary world, wars and military coups have been witnessed in nations that are endowed with mineral resources such as gold and oil. Examples of such nations are Democratic Republic of Congo and Nigeria where military coups have been witnessed partly because of the presence of oil, gold and other valuable natural resources in the ecosystem. But nations such as Kenya where there are no valuable minerals such as gold, copper, uranium and coal, there were no powerful empires and kingdoms as was the case in Ghana (Old Ghana) or South Africa (Shaka Kingdom). Most Kenyan communities were governed by a council of elders possibly because the only valuable natural resource is land. Kagwiria Orina (2018) observes that the Ameru people were ruled by a council of elders; she adds:

> The Meru people are a community living on the fertile agricultural north and eastern slopes of Mount Kenya, in the former Eastern Province of Kenya. As for many years, there was only one geo-political district for Meru people that originated from the colonial land unit. This changed in 1992, when the district was divided into three namely Meru, Nyambene and Tharaka Nithi. (p. 3)

In this passage the Meru live in an agriculturally potential area where they practice crop growing. The Agricultural potential of this region prompted the colonial government to declare Meru a part of the White Highlands to be exploited by the white settlers. One interesting thing about Kagwiria's study is the assertion that Meru were ruled by Njuri Njeki, a council of elders. The ecological conditions of Meru dictate the choice of economic activities such as crop farming, of which intellectual demand possibly contribute to the type of leadership style. The crop farmer has to think and choose acceptable farming methods that can tend the crop to fruition. For this reason, the type of leadership style chosen by crop farmers differs from that which is chosen by the pastoralist who loiters the wilderness with beasts. In Ngugi's *The River Between*, it is evident that the ecological conditions of the Agikuyu community compel characters to opt for the council of elders instead of monarchy or dictatorship.

Chege, Waiyaki's father is one of the most revered elder in Kameno and the writer says of him:

The other elders feared and respected him. For he knew, more than any other person, the ways of the land and the hidden things of the tribe. He knew the meaning of every ritual and every sign. So, he was at the head of every important ceremony. (p. 3)

This excerpt underscores the pertinent role of knowledge in Chege's community unlike military acumen among pastoralist communities. The knowledge in Chege's community includes the religious and medicinal significance of animals and plants in the community. The use of the phrase "he knew the ways of the land" underscores the nexus between the ecological environment and the culture of the people. Indeed Ngugi emphasizes the spiritual connection of the people and the land. For one to be an elder, they have to have insight and expound on the relationship between ecological features (Mount Kirinyaga, the Muguma Tree) and the spiritual aspects of the people. Waiyaki therefore desired the revered position of his father, an elder, and "... knowing all the ways of the land from Agu and Agu, long ago" (p. 6). Knowledge is essential to an elder because he or she is a counsellor, a doctor and a leader. Besides political matters, the elder will advise others in all issues with regards to religion, health; animal and crop husbandry. It is interesting to note that among the Agikuyu, these four issues are connected to ecological conditions because their land, Mount Kerinyaga, is highly cherished. Chege tells Waiyaki that very first thing God (Murungu) gave Gikuyu and Mumbi (the first parents) was land. Murungu told them, "[t]his land I give to you, O man and woman. It is yours to rule and till, you and your posterity" (p. 1). Knowledge is therefore based on exploration of God given land to make discoveries. As an elder, Chege knows the medicinal value of the different trees and the political threats meant to take the land, a spiritual gift to the people. In the sacred groove, he tells Waiyaki the medicinal value of the different trees (p. 9) and the ancient prophecy. The latter is a revelation of threats to the land, which will impoverish the community. Elders were therefore respected for their knowledge and wisdom rather than brawn and military strength to bolster democratic style of governance.

Citing Kenyatta (1938), Veronica Kimani (2010) avers that there is a nexus between crop farming and the leadership style among the Agikuyu. He writes:

> Agikuyu were ruled by an authoritarian 'king' who could not allow people to cultivate or clear the land. Therefore, the people organized a revolt led by the aregi (revolters) who formed the iregi group. After the iregi group came the ndemi (cutters) who cut trees and cleared bushes in order to cultivate. This revolution came to be known as itwika (to break away). (p. 38)

In this passage, Kimani suggests that authoritarian styles of leadership is not apt for crop farmers who have to be allotted their own pieces of land to cultivate. The authoritarian king could allot and allow the Agikuyu the land for cultivation and so the people rebelled, overthrew the dictator and appointed a council of elders to lead them. Being crop farmers, they preferred a council of elders because decisions could be made after discussion. Kimani adds, that "Agikuyu were a decentralized community where decisions were made through consensus of the people especially the council of elders" (37). Reason and persuasion, rather than brawn therefore take precedence among crop farmers. This partially arises from the need for laws that govern land ownership to facilitate effective crop growing unlike pastoralists who just roam from place to place without regard for the neighbour's property. Citing Leaky (1977), Kimani asserts that even Muthamaki, the leader of the council of elders could not make unilateral decisions, but would consult others (p. 38). This is possibly why in spite of Chege and Mugo's spiritual gifts, they are rejected by other elders, and subsequently the Agikuyu people. As crop growers, the Agikuyu people cherish the ability to reason rather than Chege and Mugo's unilateral declarations. In fact, the people associate the prevailing environmental degradation with the unilateral decisions of Christians and colonialists. The narrator says, "[i]n the past few years things were changing; the pattern of seasons was broken. It no longer rained regularly. The sun seemed to shine for months and the grass dried. And when it fell, the rainwater carried away the soil. The soil no longer answered the call and prayers of the people. Perhaps it had to do with the white men and the blaspheming men of Makuyu (p. 51). The narrator suggests that the colonialists and Christians such as Joshua elevate despotism, which results in homocentric decisions with regards to land use. Such decisions have led to deforestation and other homocentric decisions which accentuate environmental degradation. The narrator is nostalgic about traditional modes of governance that uphold consultation in order to make decisions that elevate environmental conservation.

For instance, when Chege tells the people that the white people have already taken the Agikuyu land in Murang'a, Kiambu and Nyeri the people reason out:

> "How do you know?"
>
> "See them, the butterflies."
>
> "Butterflies? You have never left the ridges!"
>
> "They are there, beyond the ridges, putting up many houses and some taking the land."
>
> [...] And they lowered their voices and
>
> whispered together:
>
> "The white man cannot speak the language of the hills."
>
> "And knows not the ways of the land." (p. 3)

In this passage, it is evident that the Agikuyu people are averse to declarations from their leaders including the wisest of elders, for instance prophets. Although Chege is a seer and is endowed with ability to perceive the advent of Europeans from the spiritual perspective, the people question how he comes to know it. They wonder how he comes to this knowledge yet he seldom leaves the ridges. They also wonder how the white people will affect the Agikuyu when they do not know their language. The Agikuyu people treasure reason so much that even prophets cannot impose decisions on them. When Waiyaki matures the people revere him and appoint him to join the new *kiama* (council of elders) to serve as a clerk (p. 41), but this does not mean Waiyaki will impose his will on the people. As Kimani contends, Waiyaki will only make decisions by consulting other elders such as Kabonyi (p. 38). Indeed when Wayaki tries to impose his belief in the centrality of formal education in Kameno, he meets opposition typical of parliamentary democracy. In the song, Waiyaki teaches the pupils, they elevate formal education over political liberation of the people from colonialism. The pupils of Marioshoni Primary school sing:

> Father,
>
> The war of shields and spears
>
> Is now ended
>
> What is left?
>
> The battle of wits,
>
> The battle of the mind.
>
> I, we, all want to learn. (p.17)

These ideas do not please some elders because colonialists have alienated the land in Kameno and Makuyu and Waiyaki should consult to elders to find ways to resist the encroachment. Kabonyi challenges him to an intellectual duel, which compels Waiyaki to give cogent reasons for his stand on the matter. The argument between Waiyaki and Kabonyi cannot be found in dictatorial communities, for instance the ilarinkon in Kulet's *Blossoms of the Savannah*. Kabonyi outlines reasons why Waiyaki has erred with regards to the leadership of the community to persuade the people to reject his opinion. After Waiyaki's speech on the need to fund the school for more teachers, desks and schools, Kabonyi:

> ....reminded them of the poverty of the land. The dry months had left the people with
>
> nothing to eat. And the expected harvest would not yield much. He touched on the land
>
> taken by the white man. He talked of the new taxes being imposed on the people by the Government Post now in their midst. And instead of Waiyaki leading people against these more immediate ills, he was talking of more buildings. Were people going to be burdened with more buildings? With more teachers? And was the white man's education really necessary? (p. 17)

This speech is very much similar to those given by members of parliament on the opposition side of the house. While Waiyaki stands for the status quo, Kabonyi overturns the conventions and demands for freedom of the African peoples. He interrogates the ideas being peddled by colonialists and also appeals to people through their proverbs and idioms. He teaches on the question of land and its central role on the economic and spiritual life of the Agikuyu people. For the community that believes the first gift which Murungu (God) gave to them was their land, it is unreasonable to substitute it with education as Waiyaki tries to. The people actually need spears and shields to liberate their land from colonial invaders. For Waiyaki, the children had to acquire formal education or risk being left behind by other communities that were imbibing the new knowledge for the West. He underscores the importance of acquiring knew knowledge. Whereas Kabonyi emphasizes the need to be led by adults, Waiyaki replies that he does not want to lead, but serve the ridges. "The elders were there to guide and lead the youth. And youth had to listen" (p. 61). The people are moved by Waiyaki's words and choose him instead of Kabonyi. This is the essence of democracy, election of leaders on the basis of their ability, knowledge and capabilities.

3.6. Hot Deserts and Dictatorial Regimes: Military Regimes in Contemporary Works of fiction

Siad Barre was born in Shilabo, Ethiopia, in 1910 to a nomadic family from the Marehan clan. He spent his formative years attending school in Luuq, Italian Somaliland, and Mogadishu for his secondary education. He later joined the colonial police force. After Somalia gained independence in July of 1960, Barre became the Vice Commander of the Somali National Army.

Ahmed S. (2021, p. 1)

Many countries in hot areas of the world tend to have dictatorial and monarchical systems of government. From Somalia, Egypt, Sudan, Libya, Algeria all the way to Saudi Arabia have had either autocratic or monarchical systems of government. In the above quote, Ahmed Sundus (2021) traces the origin of Siad Barre, the dictator of Somalia from a nomadic family. The mention of nomadism is an indirect reference to the ecological environment and its influence of the economic activities and cultural aspects of the people. Ahmed suggests that the hot and dry ecological conditions contributed to the kind of person Barre becomes. Ornas and Salih (1989) observe, "[m]ore than 90% of the Ogaden receives less than 300 mm of annual rainfall. Hence, it is clear that the three areas of political conflict are located in zones of rainfall scarcity" (p. 41). Ornas and Salih suggest that hostile environmental conditions provide a fertile ground for political violence and dictatorship is one of the causes of violence. While tracing the history of nomadism, Kradin (2016) observes, "[t]he nomads were forced into long and active contact with more highly organized agricultural urban societies (Scythians and old oriental and ancient states; nomads of Inner Asia and China). Nomadic empires were organized in the form of "imperial confederations." From the outside, these confederations appeared autocratic and state [...] but from the inside were consultative and tribal" (p.4). Kradin clarifies two things: first, crop farmers are organized and live in urban areas; second, nomads are autocratic and tribal. It is the contention of this subsection that the ecological conditions in which the nomads live contribute to their autocratic attributes. This subchapter investigates the impact of the ecological conditions on autocracy in Hisham Matar's *The Return* and Mohamed's *Orchard of Lost Souls*.

The character, President in Mohamed's *Orchard of Lost Souls* grew up in the semi-arid conditions of Somalia that expose him to nomadism. Indeed as Kradin suggests, the nomadic lifestyle inculcates autocracy in him. The narrator says:

> The President is a giant, a god who watches over them, who can dissolve into pieces and hear and see all that they do. The young nomadic boy who knew how to hobble a camel and ease a tick out of a sheep's flesh has become a

deity. A blasphemer, thinks Kawsar as his face floats up at her, both he and his servant Haaruun. (18-19)

The comparison to the deity is snide reference to Barre's autocratic tendencies that turn each of his word into law, which elevates his intolerance to opposition and criticism. Nadifa, mentions his nomadism while growing up and how the practice is devoid of reason and tender care typical of crop growing. The Somali just has to preoccupy themselves with one simple act: "hobble" a camel." The sole empathetic act they are capable of is pluck a teak out of a sheep, which is an indifferent act of taking the tick's life. The president's life in the Nadifa (2013) takes the autocratic trajectory that Kradin elucidates in his work. This begins when he schemes the assassination of a democratically elected president. Kawsar says,

> "[h]e had slipped into power almost unseen following the assassination of the last elected president and his voice when it appeared on the radio was always ominous to her; it took her back to those five days in sixty-nine after the president had been shot dead by his bodyguard and Radio Hargeisa broadcasted Qu'ranic recitations non-stop" (123).

Barre, the president in the novel, arranged the assassination of the legitimate president assumed the reigns, ending democracy in Somalia and starting a totalitarian regime that suited his nomadic lifestyle.

Similarly, Qaddafi in Matar's *The Return*, overthrows a monarchical regime of King Idris to introduce a system that suits his nomadic lifestyle in Libya. According to historical sources, "Qaddafi was born in a tent in the Libyan desert" (para 1). The tent in which he was born symbolizes the nomadic lifestyle of his parents in the desert which in Kradis perspective make him vulnerable to callous tendencies. Indeed he overthrows King Idris and establishes revolutionary committee that hunt down and kill dissidents. Matar observes that the committees "hanged students in front of Benghazi cathedral and from the gates of universities" (p.36). The president in Mohamed's *Orchard of Lost Souls* schemes wicked acts against school children. When they demonstrate against injustices, the president ordered for their arrest and detention to serve as "assets" that supply blood during the war. The narrator writes:

> The children's bodies are brought out of the anteroom in twos. A hand drops off the trolley as lifeless and yellow as an autumn leaf. Filsan watches mesmerised as the nurses go in and out of the bleeding room with barely a flicker of reaction. They hold scarlet bags of blood in their fingers – apparently destined for the operating theatre – and go around the ward with smiles for the patients. Follow orders. Follow orders. Follow orders. (p. 197)

Filsan is profoundly shocked to learn that the children have been bled to death as ascertained by the "lifeless and yellow" aspect of the hands. The nurses walk out of the rooms with "scarlet bags of blood" that is used to resuscitate the health of wounded soldiers. The nurses are so acclimatised to the evils of the dictatorship that they have no qualms about its excesses. Theirs is to "follow orders" of the totalitarian regime of which tenders has been shredded by both hostile weather and political strife.

Qaddafi in Matar's *The Return* commits similar acts on prisoners who protest against maltreatment in detention. The prisoners protest that they do not have even animal rights (266) and Sennussi, Qaddafi's henchman glibly reminds them of their marginal positionality in the Libyan political sphere. He shouts: "[w]e are government and you are prisoners. If we want, we can tonight send fighter jets to bomb the entire prison with you and the guards in it" (266). The opposition from Adjdabiya-Hisham's father's village are asked to identify themselves: Ali, Mohamoud and Ahmed do so, but Hisham's father does not. They are separated and the rest (including Hisham's father) are taken to an open yard. Hmad narrates:

> A few seconds later, we heard a loud explosion, then dense and unceasing gunfire-all sorts of weapons, machine guns and the sound of men screaming all coming from the workshop [...] it turned out that Abdullah Sennussi had initiated the massacre by throwing a hand grenade into the workshop. The shooting lasted for two hours. (269)

This happens at Abu Salim Prison where 1,270 prisoners, including Hisham's father, Jaballa Matar were massacred. Their political otherness does not even warrant a respectful interment. Their bodies were buried where they fell in shallow mass graves. To demonstrate the regimes hate for the political other, the bodies are exhumed, ground to dust and powder and poured into the sea (270). The message hits Hisham with incredible pain as it confirms the futility of his efforts to find his father.

In the same way, the doctors in *Orchard of Lost Souls* organise clean up in Hargeisa Hospital as a response to the negligence and inefficiencies of the autocratic regime. Instead of responding positively to the doctor's constructive criticism, Barre responds by sentencing all the ten doctors to death. The Maryam says, "[t]hey have sentenced all the doctors to death and now the students have gone wild" (114). The students who reckon that the government will extend some mercy at them are proved wrong when the Barre orders the police to shoot them. The narrator says, "[p]rotestors had been shot and killed near the courthouse" (114) and the students who protest in their defence are detained and bled to death as before mentioned.

> Similarly, Qaddafi hangs university students at university gates and traffic diverted towards these "guillotines" to ensure commuters see the dangling corpses. Matar adds that books and musical instruments that are deemed anti-revolutionary were confiscated from shops, schools and homes and torched. Intellectuals, union leaders, and students were shown in TV sitting handcuffed on the floor dictating confessions to the camera (p. 36).

The police have been trained by dictators in the two novels to be callous and poised to murder suspects. In *Orchard of lost Souls*, the police torture Kawsar, a helpless widow for her attempt to save Deqo from the Guddi. Filsan, though a police woman has been trained to follow the orders by the dictator to the letter. While beating Kawsar, the narrator says, "[t]he blows came one after the other. The first to her ear as a loud as a wave hitting a rock, then her temple, cheek [...] a punch to the chest knock her from the chair onto the cement" (p.35). Kawsar is terribly immobilized by the heavy blows and ends up in hospital for months. In the same way, Qaddafi sends out the police against many dissidents without his nation. A renowned Libyan economist who was stepping off a train at Stazione Termini in Rome is assassinated by Qaddafi's spy. The man "[p]ressed a pistol on his chest and pulled a trigger," (5). A Libyan student sitting on a terrace of a café in Monastiraki Square in Greece is shot dead (5-6) and a Libyan British Broadcasting Service newsreader is killed in London (6). Hisham's brother Ziad terminates his studies in Switzerland and returns to Cairo in fear of Libyan spies. For those offering "an *other*" vision for Libya, mental anguish, fear and constant reminder of the dispensability of their lives lead to psychic damage.

The autocratic political system has affected family life such that some victims resort to singleness hence obstructing the perpetuation of the family line. Filsan in Mohamed's *Orchard of Lost Souls* is adversely affected by her father's autocracy that she loses the ability to feel; hence cannot fall in love. Autocracy in Filsan's family takes Njogu and Mazrui (2013)'s view that some African communities that practiced crop farming embraced matrilineality, but patriarchy pervaded pastoralist communities (p. 4). Kadrin suggests that the patriarchal tradition in pastoralist communities is closely associated with autocracy. Indeed Filsan's father forbids her from any social life and when he finds her chatting with boys such as Abdurahman, he assaults her physically:

> You scorpion, you whore, you don't deserve to carry my name or my father's. You were going to bring those boys,

those dogs into my house? You thought while your uncle was here that you could do what you liked? Idiot! I should throw you out! [...] His blows were losing their force and he turned to sharp slaps instead, his untrimmed nails sometimes catching her skin. 'Get up to your room,' he panted and pushed her up the stairs. 'Intisaar! Check her underwear. If you find anything pack her bags and put her out.' (p. 153)

The scorpion is a desert insect with a poisonous sting, and its reference is Filsan's father's projection of his own weaknesses. He is the scorpion that silently stings Filsan with his patriarchal parenting to render her incapable of tending her womanhood. The callous natural environment and the subsequent nomadism have compelled Filsan's father to know violence as the sole means to instilling discipline in the family. The autocratic element of nomadism that Kradin suggests manifest through the violence that Filsan's father metes out on his daughter in the excerpt. It is shocking how "his blows were losing their force and he turned to sharp slaps instead" without any tender feelings for the daughter whose mother he divorced years ago. Despite the infibulation he has imposed on her, he still orders the servant to check her underwear to confirm if she has had pre-marital sex.

With the lapse of time, it is apparent that the autocratic patriarchal parenting denies Filsan her womanhood. For example, she says that she is too rational to truly love someone (164), and it embarrasses her just to see "canoodling couples." Her mother notes these symptoms and concludes, "[s]he doesn't look like the marrying kind" (165). After joining the military, Filsan is confounded to realize that she is single in spite of being ripe for marriage. In her low moments, Filsan blames her father for "locking her" away from social life, which leads her to "a celibate, sterile, quiet existence of a nun, growing nothing, but grey hairs" (p.138). This assertion proves that Filsan is not happy with her singleness.

In Matar's *The Return*, the prevalent dictatorship compels characters to a life of nomadism and migration; living like single people. Grandfather Ahmed and Jaballa are such examples. When Hisham reads his father's short story, he discovers that he suffered a lot as result of Grandfather Ahmed's absence from home. Hisham describes Jaballa's short story as "a fictional vessel into which the eighteen year old author could deposit his worst fears" (142). Jaballa's father (Grandfather Ahmed) joins the resistance movement to liberate Libya from Italian colonizers and he is deported to remote Islands in Italy. His son Jaballa is abandoned to live as a destitute. In the story, he writes, "I wandered aimlessly and did not find anywhere that would take me except that one place that had absorbed thousands of miserable souls: the street" (142). Jaballa's life, like Filsan's in Mohamed's *Orchard of Lost Souls* is "sterile and growing nothing" (p. 138). Hisham comments that his father's struggle against prevalent dictatorship has devastating consequences on his social life, that is, loss of "family, his home—until he is left destitute" (p. 142). Later, as Hmad narrates, Jaballa is one of those massacred in prison after many years of incarceration, away from family (269).

From the foregoing discussion, most communities living in arid or desert regions practice nomadic pastoralism and have had autocratic governments. Countries such as Somalia, Libya, Egypt, Algeria and Saudi Arabia have mostly been ruled by dictatorial regimes because of the prevailing ecological conditions that contribute to the choice of such systems of governments. As Kradin contends, democracy has not been a choice of leadership styles among nomads and this is possibly why it has always flopped in Egypt and Afghanistan. The so called democratic Mohamed Mursi's regime was overthrown by the Egyptian army in less than a year without complaints from the US, a bastion of democracy. After twenty-one years of American rule, democracy could not take root in Afghanistan and Americans abandoned the weak democratic regime to be dethroned in less than six months by the autocratic Taliban. The ecological conditions therefore contributes to the system of government chosen people in a region.

REFERENCES

Ahmed S. (2021). Mohammed Siad Barre. *Blackpast*.

https://www.blackpast.org/global-african-history/people-global-african-history/mohamed-siad-barre-1910-1995/.

Angeles, L. (2013) On the causes of the African slave trade. Kyklos, 66 (1). pp. 1-26.

Bhat A. (2016). Utilitarianism in Hard Times: An Education Perspective. IJAR, 4.11: p 2391-

23-97. https://www.researchgate.net/publication/311778347_UTILITARIANISM_IN_HARD_TIMES_AN_EDUCATIONAL_PERSPECTIVE.

Brown D. (2018). Barbaric': America's cruel history of separating children from their parents. Retropolis. https://www.washingtonpost.com/news/retropolis/wp/2018/05/31/barbaric-americas-cruel-history-of-separating-children-from-their-parents/.

Churchill, Lord R. (1897) Men, Mines and Animals in South Africa. 1892. New ed. London: Sampson, Low and Marston.

Constable G. A. Temperature Requirements for Cotton. *NSW Agriculture and Fisheries.*

https://www.dpi.nsw.gov.au/__data/assets/pdf_file/0003/710796/Agfact-P5.3.5-Temperature-requirements-for-cotton.pdf.

Cussen, C., Manuel Llorca-Jaña and Federico Droller (2016). The dynamics and determinants of slave prices in an urban setting: santiago de chile, c. 1773-1822. *Journal of Iberian and Latin American Economic History.* 1: 1-29. doi:10.1017/S0212610915000361.

Guma, L. A. (1972). *In the Fog of a Season's End.* Nairobi: EAEP.

Jacobs, H. (1861). *Incidents in the Life of Slave Girl.* Penguin Books.

Kagwiria, O (2018). The contributions of councils of elders to the resilience of African traditional religion: a case of njuri ncheke in meru county, kenya. MA Thesis, Egerton University.

Koponen J. (1993). The Partition of Africa: A Scramble for a Mirage? *Nordic Journal of African Studies* 2.1: 117–135. http://www.njas.helsinki.fi/pdf-files/vol2num1/koponen.pdf.

Karari, Peter (2018). Modus Operandi of Oppressing the "Savages": The Kenyan British

Colonial Experience. *Peace and Conflict Studies*: 25 : p. 1-16. https://nsuworks.nova.edu/pcs/vol25/iss1/2.

Kimani, V. (2010). The transformation of Circumcision and Masculinity among the

Agikuyu of Kiambu, 1945-2008. MA Thesis Kenyatta University. https://ir-library.ku.ac.ke/bitstream/handle/123456789/13383/The%20Transformation%20of%20Circumcision....pdf;sequence=1.

Kradin N. (2016). Nomads. *Russian Academy of Sciences and Far-Eastern FederalUniversity, Russia*.DOI:10.1002/9781118455074.wbeoe171.https://www.researchgate.net/publication/314837281_Nomads.

Muamar Qaddafi. *Britanica*. https://www.britannica.com/biography/Muammar-al-Qaddafi.

Miguelanez B. (2015). *Dickens on the industrial revolution*.

https://core.ac.uk/download/pdf/211099292.pdf.

Mulwa, D. (2004). *Inheritance*. Nairobi: Loghorn.

Ngugi, W. T. (1967). *A Grain of Wheat*. Nairobi: EAEP.

Oliver, E. & Oliver, W.H., (2017). The Colonisation of South Africa: A unique case.

Theological Studies, 73.3: p.2-8. http://www.scielo.org.za/pdf/hts/v73n3/62.pdf.

Ornas A. and Salih M. (1989). *Ecology and Politics: Environmental Stress and Security in Africa.* Motala: Scandinavian Institute of African Studies.

Sesay A. (2014). African Governance Systems in the Pre and Post-Independence Periods:

Enduring Lessons and Opportunities for Youth in Africa. *Centre for Peace and Strategic Studies.* https://minds-africa.org/Downloads/Youth%20Dialogue%202014%20Research%20p.

Liden, G. (2014). Theories of Dictatorships: Sub-Types and Explanations, Studies *of Transition States and Societies* 6.1. http://miun.diva-portal.org/smash/get/diva2:731017/FULLTEXT01.pdf.

Verhenye, W. ( ). Growth and production of sugarcane. *Growth and Production of Sugarcane.* http://www.eolss.net/sample-chapters/c10/e1-05a-22-00.pdf.

Smith W. (2003). The Boers and the Anglo-Boer war (1899–1902) in the twentieth-century moral Imaginary. *Victorian Literature and Culture*, 31. 2: p.429- 445.

Warnick B. (2008). Oppression, Freedom and Education of Frederic Douglass. *Philosophical Studies in Education* 39: p. 25-34.

Williams, E. (1944), Capitalism and Slavery, University of North Carolina Press.

Udofia, J. (2013). The Shaping and History of Caribbean Literature. *American Journal of Humanities and Social Sciences*, 1, 2:p 56-62

Chapter Four

Mother Nature and Religion: Ecological Environment and Belief Systems in Contemporary Novels

Among the Akan, the whole Earth is sacred, and any place can be a place for worship. Mother Earth, therefore, is a sacred space. (p. xiii)

Mercy Oduyoye (2020)

Great religions of the world, for example Christianity and Islam base their origin on revelation that emanates from homocentric attributes such as seclusion, fasting and prayer. From Biblical and Koranic texts, both founders of Judaism, Christianity and Islam spent many hours of fasting to access the creator of life. Other indigenous religions however reject this homocentric worldview and extract their religious beliefs from their ecological settings. Oduyoye's study of the Akan indigenous religion supports this thesis because they place Mother Nature at their very centre of religious worship. The whole earth is holy altar that should be treated with caution to evade retribution from the supernatural.

The Akan belief system is quite similar to the Yoruba and ancient Egyptian religions that drew some of their deities from the ecological environment. In his study of Yoruba religion, Hall (1917) writes:

> The highest—also the most remote—of the gods is Olorun. He is a vaguely conceived god of the sky, whom no one worships nor heeds. Why should they, since he himself takes no heed of men's affairs? The other gods are nearer to men, forefathers of the people, controlling forces useful to their posterity, whom therefore these have it at heart to placate by offerings, and to honor by worship. Such are Obatala, whom Olorun begot, and to whom he has handed over the management of the firmament and the earth; Shango, the thunder-god; Ogun, god of iron; Shankpanna, the small-pox god; Edshu, god of strife and bringer of the Ifa oracle to men. (p. 55)

The choice of deities is drawn from the ecological environment, for example Olorun is the god of the sky, and he is ignored because the sky is not on Mother Earth. This means the Yoruba have no time for religion that is of no earthly use. Religion, for them must be in touch with the affairs of human beings. Obatala is therefore appreciated and appeased with sacrifices because he keeps the firmament of the earth in place. Shango is also poplar because he is the god of thunder, which can cause destruction when it rains heavily. Ogun is the god of iron and is worshipped because iron is common in the community. Shankpanna is concerned with smallpox that is common in the community. In the same way, the Egyptian religion was based on what existed in the ecological environment. The Pharaoh, the King was one of the gods that has organized society to bring peace and order. He is Horus:

> The hero/king who establishes, embodies and updates the social world is also the same force that establishes, embodies and updates the intrapsychic world, the personality—and that one act of update cannot necessarily or reasonably be distinguished from the other. In improving' the world, the hero improves himself; in improving himself, he sets an example to the world. (Richards B., 2020, p. 9)

According to Richards, Egyptian religion is based on what is around the people, for instance the Pharaoh and the courageous acts he has done to unite the people under his laws. Pharoah is described as a person who "sets an example to the world or Egyptians around." This shows that for Egyptians, for the ecosystem to be stable, human life must be organised under leadership. Osiris is described as the god of fertility, which replenishes Mother Earth with new offspring for continuity.

In chapter Four, I focus on the nexus between the ecological environment and religious aspects of characters in selected works of prose. The subchapters demonstrate how Mother Nature influences traditional religions in selected works of prose. The texts include Ngugi Wa Thiong'os *The River Between*, Farah's *Secrets*, Mohamed's *Black Mamba Boy* and Witi Ihimera's *The Whale Rider*.

4.1 Mother Nature and the Patriarch: The Sea and the First Man in Ihimera's *The Whale Rider*

As discussed before, most world religions hold a homocentric view concerning the origin of the humankind, particularly Judaism, Christianity and Islam. However, among the Maori of New Guinea, Mother Nature holds the greatest sway with regards to the origin of humanity. Whereas in Judaism, Christianity and Islam, the first man was created by a person or supernatural being, among the Maori, the first man arose from what Mother Nature already possessed: The Sea and the Whales. Ihimera contends that before the origin of the first man among the Maori, Mother Nature was already in existence. He writes:

> In the old days, in the years that have gone before us, the land and sea felt great emptiness, a yearning. The mountains were like a stairway to heaven and the lush green forest was a rippling cloak of many colours. The sky was iridescent, swirling with the patterns of wind and clouds; sometimes it reflected the prisms of rainbow or southern aurora. The sea was ever changing, shimmering and seamless to the sky…this was not to say the land and sea were without life, without vivacity. The Tuatara, the ancient Lizard with its third eye was sentinel here, unblinking in the hot sun. (p. 2)

The land and the sea therefore existed before the origin of the first man. The mountains were existent like staircases poised to lead people to the heaven, but without such persons to use them. The narrator adds that the emptiness of Mother Nature does not suggest its lifelessness, there was life even before the advent of humankind. We have the ancient Lizard, Tuatara that enjoys the hot sun. The Maori religion therefore inverts the modern homocentric views that otherize Mother Nature in favour of humankind. This is similar to the Christian story of creation in that humankind appears as the last element of creation. Whereas, Adam is created to rule over Mother Nature, among the Maori, humankind is created to serve Mother Nature. The narrator says before the existence of humankind, "earth and sea began to feel the sharp pangs need" (p. 3). As Bacon suggests in the introduction, the earth and the sea hungered for a servant, not a master. Ihimera further demonstrates how the first man emerged from an offspring of Mother Nature, a whale. He writes:

> The sun rose and set, rose and set. Then one day, at its noon apex, the first sighting was made. A spume on the horizon. A dark shape rising from the greenstone depths of the ocean, awesome Leviathan, breaching through the surface and hurling itself skyward before falling seaward again [...] suddenly, the sea was filled with awesome singing, a song with eternity in it [...]. The dark shape rising, rising again. A whale, gigantic. A Sea Monster. Just as it burst through the sea, a flying fish leaping high[...]then the flying fish saw that astride the head, as it broke skyward,, was a man. The water streamed away from him and he opened his mouth to gasp in the cold air. [...]Upon the beast, he looked like a small tattooed figurine, dark brown, glistening and erect. (P. 3-4).

This extract summarises the myth of the origin of humankind among the Maori and unlike homocentric attributes of contemporary religions and modernism, the existence of humankind stems from Mother Nature's resolution to create a servant. The sun has been in existence many seasons before the sea and her offspring think about the possibility of having humankind. As soon as these existing creatures think of the possibility of having a person, the whale, "a dark shape rising from the greenstone depths of the ocean" decides to create the first man. It is described as "a Sea Monster, a gigantic whale" arising with determination to bring forth a person to assist in serving Mother Nature. The Whale casts forth a flying fish that turns in an instant into a man. The last sentence underscores the subordinate position of humankind in creation; the man is but "a small tattooed figurine, dark brown, glistening and erect" that must live according to the dictates of his creator: The Sea and the whale. This is in absolute contrast to Spedding et al. assertions, "[n]ature must be bound into service and made a slave, put in constraint, and moulded by the mechanical arts" (20) since the first man, Paikea has been created at Mother Nature's volition or mercy.

It is therefore apparent that among the Maori, Mother Nature dictates the fundamental beliefs of the religion. The presence of the Sea, and the creatures in it, for example the fishes and whales determine what and how they worship. Michele Canfield (2011) asserts, "Ihimaera also comments on the importance of reclaiming ancient heritage, and rediscovering and reconnecting to the sea and the creatures it sustains. The importance of these ideas directly relates to the people's survival as a tribe and the ultimate survival of Earth" (p. 42). The reference to the Maori religion reiterates the pertinent role of Mother Nature in the survival and continuation of the Maori community. The Sea and the Whale is a god of sorts, because it is through their presence that the community acquires the economic means of sustenance. Whereas Canfield observes that the Maori patriarch "came riding through the sea astride his whale, and he brought with him the life-giving forces which would enable us to live in close communion with the world" (p. 44), this subchapter takes the authentic description given in the Maori myth of creation that the ancestor was created by the "gingatic whale." As a result, the Maori religious system evolves around absolute reverence for Mother Nature. Marilyne Arwood (2015) in her article about Maori beliefs writes:

> While most religions place their god as the creator of the world, the Maori, by worshiping the two primary gods Papatuanuku (the earth mother) and Ranginui (the sky father), place their gods directly in and on the planet, acknowledging the holiness and value of nature itself. These two main gods are the parents of mankind; therefore the humans have a relationship with the world in which they inhabit. Overusing the resources that are available on the earth damages this relationship between the earth and man. Parents will care for their children and protect them, but the children need to show respect and care as well. (Para 3)

The Maori therefore find the creator of the earth within the ecological environment as she sustains their physical existence. Like the Akan, mentioned in Oduyoye's study, the Maori acknowledge the sanctity of Mother Nature and all the things in her possession. In the relationship between Nature and humankind, the former is the parent and humankind the child expected to behave responsibly or suffer the wrath of the parent if they misbehave. As a result of this ecological consciousness, Arwood observes that the Maori exhibit great care for their ecological environment. She says that "[w]hen you go through customs, the harshest fines are attached to bringing in any kind of plant or bacteria that may damage the ecosystem" (para, 1). In the same way, Koro Apirana in Ihimera's *The Whale Rider* is apprehensive about the flipside of the recklessness of the young generation with regards to environmental conservation. The homocentric philosophy characteristic of the modern age has resulted to over whaling that threatens the very existence of Maori Culture. The Maori are confounded by foreign fishing companies that elevate this over exploitation. The narrator says:

> Five men are working on the whale. They are splattered with blood. As the helicopter hovers above them, one of the men stops his work and smiles directly into the camera. The look is triumphant. He lifts his arms in a victory sign and the camera focuses on other men, where they stand in the surging water. The chainsaw has just completed cutting through the whale's lower jaw. The men are laughing as they wrench the jaw from the butchered whale. There is a huge spout of blood as the jaw suddenly snaps free. […]Blood, laughing, pain, victory, blood. (p. 80)

These modern poachers are not simply viewed as hunters of whales, but in fact apostates of the Maori religion since their whales are gods that form the very foundation of the Maori religion. While one of the poachers exhibits triumphant feelings over Nature, the

Maori onlookers sympathize at the man's vulnerability to the spiritual consequences of their god. As Arwood argues, Nature is a parent, and one who harms as these men do expects nothing, but a parental retribution or curse that will lead them to damnation. The Maori witnesses arrive at the scene and threaten the poachers with whatever they lay their hands on. The community seeks for help to save the whale and subsequent curse from the divine. According to Dionne L. (2006), the beaching scene is filled "with descriptions of machinery and technology that do not permeate the rest of the text: vehicles, from helicopters to trucks to heavy construction equipment; chain saws, television crews, radio broadcasts, newspapers" (p. 69) because it transgresses the traditional views of the Maori with regards to Nature. In other words, the modern homocentric world view is an adversary to the ecological environment.

The actual Maori belief system elevates Mother Nature to the divine status and therefore a number of religious rites have to be performed to appease their god (which are closely tied to Mother nature). For example, whenever humankind wants to move towards the ocean, "he would honour Tangaroa by making offerings of Sea weed, fish or birds" (p. 32). Tangaroa is the patriarch of the Maori community, who, although honoured for being the first person, it's the whale that created him that is revered in this offering. Furthermore, when a fisherman had sufficient catch, he had to appreciate the Sea god by returning "the first fish of the catch" back to the sea. The Sea god, from the myth of creation, is the bull whale that took the initiative to bring Paikea into being.

Moreover, when they need the Sea god's favour, they make offerings to him to thank him. Before fishing, "we have blessed every new net and new line to Tangaroa" (p. 38). Having derived his existence from the bull Whale, any effort to appease Tangaroa is a way to appease the whale and Mother Nature. It is therefore the worship of Mother Nature for her determination to sustain the Maori community by her fish and Sea Creatures. They do not carry along their food while fishing "because of the sacred nature of our task" (p. 38). The fishing areas are protected by the guardians to ensure that all religious rules are adhered. In honour of these fishing grounds, Koro Apirana says:

> We have often placed talismanic shrines. In this way, the fish have been protected and attracted to the fishing grounds, and thus a plentiful supply has been assured. We try never to overfish, for to do so would be to take greedy advantage of Tangaroa and would bring retribution. (P.38)

Mother Nature has to be handled with reverence to ensure constant supply for sustenance. For Nature of the Sea god that Apirana talks of; without the Sea, the whale would not have survived; subsequently, the bull whale would not have created the patriarch. Overfishing would violate the very sea that so mercifully created man. For the Maori, Nature made man, and he has to live by her whims. She creates, she sustains: he is created, he is nourished. He must stick to the conventions she has set or perish.

The sanctity of the Sea was upheld given its initial role in the creation of Man; subsequently, "fishing was sacred and women therefore did not go out with men, and fishing grounds became steeped in special rituals to ensure their bounty" (p. 32). The men take pride in the knowledge that the whale created a man as the first representative of humankind, but forget that it is the whale's prerogative to determine its representative from generation to generation. This gender politics in Ihimera's *The Whale Rider* is another confirmation of the pre-eminence of Mother Nature over humankind.

Whereas Koro Apirana, the undisputable spiritual leader believes that only men have the gods permission to lead the community, Mother Nature, as represented by the Sea god (whale) has the last word. It is confounding to Apirana and other male chauvinists to realize that there is no other person the Sea god (whale) listens to except Kahu. Rawiri, the narrator is amazed to see Kahu talk to the whale, "[s]he was singing to the whale. Telling it to acknowledge her coming" (101). When she approaches the whale, he "felt a surge of gladness, which as it mounted, became ripples of ecstasy, ever increasing" (p. 102). Kahu speaks to the whale and he starts moving towards the open sea to ensure the survival of the community. The narrator says, "[t]he whale began to turn to the open sea... the younger whales came to push their leader into the deeper water" (p.104). The Sea god, (bull whale) recognizes their leader, in spite of her female gender, to demonstrate his pre-eminence over Apirana's human authority. Kahu executes her mission as the next priest of the religion to the embarrassment of the Apirana. The Sea god has chosen a girl to lead the community. Apirana regrets his homocentric perspective with regard to religious leadership of the community. The narrator says, "[h]e asked the gods to forgive him" (p.120). Ihimera suggests that ecological conditions have a greater role in gender relations than homocentric perspectives. Apirana gives way to Mother Nature's superiority; he tells Kahu, the girl, to "return to the people and take your rightful place among them" (p.120). When Mother Nature gives a go ahead, the gender does not matter. She dictates and humanity submits to her will.

4.2 Mother Nature and Somali Indigenous Religion: *Wagar* and the Crow in Contemporary Somali Fiction

> Alongside *haydh*, a great many additional materials are required for this ritual (wagar). The items are usually made from iron, trees and grass from sacred landscapes. Often, the shrines of Sufi saints in Somalia and Somaliland fall into this category. The aforementioned sacrificial offering was made to the shrine of the twelfth-century Saint Aw-Barkhadle, a sacred site that will be explored in greater detail below. Such landscapes and items carry multivalent symbolic meanings and suggest the appropriation of pre-Islamic traditions regarding the sacredness and power of the natural world.
>
> Mire S. (2015)

In spite of claims that associate the Somali population with the dominance of the Islamic religion, social scientists content that indigenous Somali religion was based on aspects of Mother Nature such as trees and birds. The Somali people therefore recognized the supremacy of the ecological environment and continues to practice some of these rituals in spite of the prevalence of Sunni Islam in their culture. Sada Mire (2015) in the above quote demonstrates how the Somali people create powerful charm, a concoction or mix of trees, iron, grass and other products of Nature into a powerful object that is believed to offer protection against infertility, sicknesses and invisible enemies. Mire concludes that the creation of such a charm recognises the "sacredness and power" of Mother Nature among the Somali.

This subchapter extends Mires trajectory with regard to the pre-eminence of Mother Nature on traditional Somali religion in Mohamed's *Black Mamba Boy* and Farah's *Secrets*. In the Subchapter, I seek to investigate how characters adopt aspects of Mother Nature to build a belief system for their spiritual nourishment.

The character Ambaro, Jama's mother in Mohamed's *Black Mamba Boys* reiterates Mires' argument of the worship of the Sky God among pre-Islamic Somalis. Ambaro tells her son Jama to look at the sky where stars exist. The narrator underscores the presence of the sky rather than stars: "[t]he sky was black and luminous as coal, a white hot crescent moon hung over them" (p. 44). For Ambaro, "[e]ach of those stars have a power of meanings in our lives." Through this character, Mohamed suggests that the sky held great sway in the spiritual aspects of the Somali community, and hence worshipped as a God. Mire asserts, [b]elief in the Sky-God may relate to the myth of the man who was sitting in a tree (perhaps a sacred tree, even an olive) [...] According to this myth, a little girl discovered a stranger from the sky, a man, sitting on a tree, who would only agree to come down when he was promised that he could marry the local girl who found him. He was allowed to marry her, and the people emerged from their union" (p. 106). Given that the sky produced a man and relayed him through a tree, the two elements of the ecological environment have the greatest influence of the perpetuation and sustenance of the Somali community. The stars, which inhabit this very sky may directly have been involved in the creation of this very man that descended through a tree to marry the first Somali daughter. Ambaro therefore tells her son to take treat of the stars with the gravity they deserve, "[t]hose stars are our friends, they have watched over our ancestors [...] they will watch over you, and will watch over your grandchildren" (p. 44). In the Islamic and Christian context, only a deity has the power to watch over ancestors and posterity. Mires opinion is therefore justified because Ambaro look up to the sky for blessings.

Furthermore, the belief in the protective charm that has been produced from Mother Nature's bowels. According to Somali belief, "[t]he wagar is, as established, from a sacred tree, and for this reason is used as a sacred weapon to fight not only abstract enemies such as umaddaha hoose but also flesh-and blood people"

(Mire, 2015. p. 100). This is why Ambaro gives her son, Jama a wagar amulet just before her death. She adjures him to pick the "amulet from my neck" and the narrator says, "Jama began to unpick the large knots in the string that hung the amulet over Ambaro's chest. [...] Jama squeezed the amulet in his palm" (45). His act to squeeze the amulet is a profound assurance of divine protection around him.

Related to the trees are birds and snakes that live in them and dominate as clan totems in the Somali community. In Farah's *Secrets*, the crow is the clan totem of Kalaman's, (the prime mover's) clan and appears in the home when he is born. Telling of his grandfather's narration of his birth, Kalaman says:

> The bird was contented looking as a child, excited at the prospect of going on a festive outing. The question was, would the crow go with him into the compound where Damac was having her labour pangs. Or would he fly off into the unknown, leaving behind himself a mystery, some sort of archaic link with pre-Islamic Somalia, a mythical creature elevated to the status of a deity? (p. 159)

As a totem, the crow is a deity, worshipped by Kalaman's clan and it appears mysteriously as his Mother is giving birth to him. Having appeared from the sky and trees, she symbolizes the sky god's protection over Kalaman and that is why Nnono and all around desire to see the crow inside the room where the child is being birthed. As soon as the crow leaves, another bird appears as messenger of the sky god to assign the child a name. This is the griot, which Nonno listen to as though "waiting for intimation as what was to be from Waaq, the ancient Somali sky god" (p. 161). Farah suggests that ancient Somali religion was directly linked to Mother Nature's physical attributes: the sky, the birds and trees. The griot sits on the highest branch of a Figtree and "issuing a squawk which to my grandfather's ears sounded like "Kalaman" prompted the prime mover to be so named. When the child does not cry, the crow moves closer to the room as grandfather, Nnono is allowed into the room and using a tamarind seed enables the baby to cry. As women celebrate "the crow descended from the height of his seclusion" (163) as gesture of joining the celebration. The crow exhibits its divinity as is thus described:

> The feathered creature responded to the villager's welcome and teasing in squawks of amicability demonstrably pleased. It was a though in an earlier existence he had known himself by that name, or he had known Nonno or this particular village. But a number of farmhands the idea of a crow in their midst as distasteful as kissing an object of derision. (p.163)

The crow in this birth ceremony is a person as he knows wrong, right and directs the events of the occasion in every way. He communicates with Nnono to save the child and determines the name by which he is called. Although a few villager complain of the oddity of the situation, the crow's magical presence attracts, compels the co-existence. This ascertains Mires perspective of the influence of Wagar in the Somali community. Mohamed in *Black Mamba Boy* confirms this with reference to the life of Jama in Somaliland. Like Farah, Mohamed explicitly asserts that Jama's "ancestors had been crow worshippers and sorcerers before the time of the prophet and the people still kept tokens of their paganism" (p. 49). The so called "paganism" is the religion that is based on Mother Nature: the sky, the trees and the birds.

As if to reconnect himself to the pre-Islamic faith of his people, Jama he lies under an acacia tree, and the narrator says:

> Black leather amulets hung from the chubby wrists of infants. His mother's amulet was tied as tightly as noose around his neck, the sacred pages grubby and hardened together [...] the sky covered him like a blue shroud and he felt cooled by the watery blueness washing over him. (p. 49)

The sky in this passage signifies the sky god, Waaq that Jama unconsciously appeals to for assistance after the demise of her mother in Yemen. He is forced to reconnect with his ancestral land before getting direction for his mythical, hero's journey to his destiny. The amulet, which as Mire explains is a magical object from trees, ensures Jama's spiritual immunity as he braces himself for the long journey to yonder lands. Indeed when Jama embarks on his journey from Hergeisa, Mohamed suggests that the sky god is in firm control of his journey. In spite of being cursed by her grandmother, Jinnow in her defence of the aunt, Ayan, the sky god in conjunction with Jama's deceased mother go ahead of Jama. For example when he falls in a pit on the way to Djibouti, the goblin of his mother appears in the subsequent sleep and the narrator refers to Wagar thus, "[t]he sky cracked and revealed a blue and white secret kingdom. The high heavens and low earth were joined by a sheet of conquering raindrops" (p. 74). Jama is given a rare opportunity into the spiritual Kingdom of the sky god "saw drenched jinnis cavorting and dancing as they reclaimed the desert for themselves" (p. 74). The Jinnis in this passage are good spirits that have been sent by the sky god to lead and protect Jama during the difficulty times. Although Islam upholds the belief in good Jinnis (Okasha, 2012, p. 74), it is Mother Nature pre-Islamic religion that prompts the coming of Jinnis to save Jama in the current predicament. The sky cracks and by sending the rain orders the spiritual agents to act on behalf of the god. The Jinnis leave footmarks that assist Jama come out of the pit; the narrator says, "Jama placed his feet in large foot prints that Jinnis has left behind. Left leg, right leg..." (p.74) till he is able to leave the pit. In the same way, Jama puts his trust in the sky god as he leaves Djibouti where he saw "a woman sitting on a star [...] he waved at his mother and she smiled back, blowing shooting star kisses down on him" (p. 95). His journey to destiny is therefore determined by the spiritual direction of Wagar. Similarly, Farah's heroine, Sholoongo demonstrates the pre-eminence of the sky god over human affairs. Kalaman says that she was a born a *duguun*, "a baby to be buried" (p. 2), and so her mother carried and abandoned her to die in the bush. However, the stars in the sky assumed the reins to protect and preserve Sholoongo's life. In a conversation with Kalaman, Sholoongo underscore the superiority of Mother Nature by expounding "the Milk Way...affected the weather and a person's destiny" (p. 2). Sholoongo suggests that the sky god has ordered the plot of her life and so humankind is helpless; Kalaman says "a lioness adopted and raised her together with her cubs, then abandoned her at crossroads, where some travellers found her" (p. 2). When her mother sees the baby back to her village, she commits suicide to show the helplessness of humanity before the sky god, and by extension, Mother Nature. Like Jama's experience, the homocentric belief that parents can curse children and grandchildren at their volition is rendered worthless as the sky god dispenses justice as He wishes. He gives Sholoongo powers to change herself into different animals to avenge any one she wishes.

It is the view of this subchapter that the elevation of the ecological environment results in magic and shape shifting in pre-Islamic Somali community. The admiration for wild animals compels characters to attain greater spiritual powers in Farah's *Secrets* and Mohamed's *Black Mamba Boy*. Mohamed says of some of Jama's ancestors possessing shapeshifting abilities: "nomads who at night turned into animals and looked for human prey in town, disappearing before daybreak and the first call to prayer" (p. 54). This assertion is quite similar to the earlier version that describes Jama's ancestors as "crow worshippers and sorcerers" (p.49), and one amazing observation about the magical states is their dependency on Mother Nature. The sorcerers turn into animals to accomplish their miraculous feats. Whereas Mohamed just mentions these magical aspects of Jama's ancestors, Farah in *Secrets* creates characters that constantly turn into animals to accomplish their malevolent acts to showcase their Nature centric religion.

Farah's heroine Sholoongo changes herself into an abstract image and gets into Kalaman's mother's dreams as a ratel, hoppo and elephant to terrorize her. As soon as Sholoongo comes to the village, Kalaman's mother experiences horrifying dreams with a motley of animals, "and sometimes graves desecrated, bodies dug up and buried anew" (p. 14). She has the powers to alter herself into different animals and insects. She has been at Kalamna's mother's shop without her knowledge (p. 47). She appears to his brother Timir as a maggot in a dream (p. 55). Fed up with Fidows poaching activities, Sholoongo turns herself into an elephant and tramples Fidow to death (p. 97). Days later, people says that Fidow's murderer is not an elephant, but a human being disguised as one" (p.100). The pre-Islamic Somali religion, with lots of mystic things or magic maintains a strong connection to Mother Nature. The sky, plants and animals inspire a religion that is firmly in control of humankind many centuries after the advent of religions that elevate homocentric perspectives.

4.3 The Eminence of Mother Nature: Mountain and *Mugumo* Altars in Contemporary Fiction

> Thus, 'religion' seems to have been intrinsically linked to the other aspects of their culture. It is under these parameters that they conceive of Ngai and he in return manifests himself to them. But to do this, Ngai uses the land, and as a consequence, it becomes sacrosanct. Thus, land and trees become a podium for a 'religious' interaction, participation and experience.
>
> (Mathew Karangi, 2005, p. 85)

African understanding of God is closely related to the ecological environment in which they live, which transgresses the homocentric perspective typical of Judeo-Christian and Islamic traditions that otherize Mother Nature. The ecological features form a great proportion of most African religions hence re-centring Mother Nature in the religious aspects. Mathew Karangi in the above quote demonstrates how the Agikuyu associate God with the beauty of Mount Kenya and, the trees on the mountain and other ecological features. Karangi adds that in the myth of origin, "land was a free gift from Ngai so that the Gikuyu became the first ancestor" and therefore the deity has strong connection to the land. It is sacred and the main point at which rituals are held to offer thanksgiving to Ngai. For Karangi, "land acted as a podium through which they could communicate with Ngai around the sacred Mugumo and other sacred groves spread throughout their territory" (p. 102). The presence of Mount Kenya and the tree species it provides therefore contribute to the major tenets of the Agikuyu religion.

This subchapter will focus on the influence of the ecological environment on Agikuyu religion with reference to Ngugi wa Thiong's *The River Between* and *A Grain of Wheat*. The subsection investigates the impact of ecological environment of religious aspects of the Agikuyu people.

In Ngugi's The *River Between*, the presence of the Mountain and Mogumo tree contributes to the spiritual insight of the inhabitants. When Chege takes his son to the sacred grove, the spiritual impact of the ecological features is evident. The narrator says:

A big Mugumo tree stood near the edge of the hill. It was a huge tree, thick and mysterious. Bush grew and bowed reverently around it. And there the ancient tree stood, towering over the hill, watching, as it were, the whole country. It looked holy and awesome, dominating Waiyaki's soul so that he felt very small and in the presence of a mighty power. This was a sacred tree. It was the tree of Murungu. Waiyaki, now on top of the hill, on the other side of the tree, surveyed the land. And he felt as if his heart would stop beating so overcome was he by the immensity of the land. The ridges were all flat below his small feet. To the east, the sun had already risen. It could now be seen clearly, a huge red ball of smoldering colors. Strands of yellowish-red thinned outwards from the glowing center, diffusing into the thick grey that joined the land to the clouds. Far beyond, its tip hanging in the gray clouds, was Kerinyaga. Its snow-capped top glimmered slightly, revealing the seat of Murungu. (p. 9)

The *mugumo* tree, an aspect of the ecological environment stuns Waiyaki; Ngugi suggests that the tenets of this traditional religion such as sanctity of Mugumo tree are prompted by the tree's beauty; hence the pre-eminence of Mother Nature. The tree is described as "the ancient tree, towering over the hill". Its beauty commands reverence and is therefore described as "holy and awesome". Karangi observes, "Ngai also dwells in the sacred Mugumo *(ficus thoningii/ natalensis)* tree. This big tree symbolises the mountains and thus the presence of Ngai" (p. 90). Besides the sanctity of the mugumo tree, the land mesmerizes Waiyaki because of its fertility and hence potential to sustain the community. The mountain and its snow cap at the pinnacle prompts Waiyaki to declare it the seat of Murungu or God. Ngugi describes the beauty of the land in the same way in *A Grain of Wheat* to show the magnitude of loss after land alienation. He writes:

> Situated in a central position, Mahee fed guns and ammunition to the other smaller police and military posts scattered in the Rift Valley to protect and raise the morale of white settlers. If you stood at Mahee at any time of day, you would see the walls of the escarpment, an enchanting guard to one of the most beautiful valleys in the land. The walls climbed in steps to the highlands; a row of smaller hills, some hewn round at the top while others bore scoops and volcano mouths, receded into shrouds of mist and mystery. (p. 11)

The narrator underscores the mesmerizing beauty of the land because of the walls of the escarpment that enchant and guard valleys. The walls exist in steps towards Mountains, which could be Aberdare ranges or any of the four mountains that comprise of Ngai's abode. Then there is a row of hills some extracted from the top while others bear pieces of volcanic craters. The use of the term "mystery" refers to the spiritual qualities of the land both as a sacred place for worship and deity to be worshipped. In *River Between*, Ngugi refers to the snow tip of the mountain, which amazes the Agikuyu so much that they declare the mountain the deity's home. In his thesis on Agikuyu cosmology, Karangi says that "Ngai lives in the four mountains; Mount Kenya, Kinangop in the Aberdares, *Kianjahi* in the east *Kiambiruiru* in the south and Longonot Crater in Maasai territory" (p. 93). The "volcano mouth" in *A Grain of Wheat* is a reference to Mount Longonot crater that posits one of the most beautiful sights in the world. Karang observes:

> Mount Kenya is believed to be the cardinal of all the mountains in Kenya, is exceptionally high. It is 5199 m above sea level and the second highest mountain in Africa. Thus its height is impressive with its three snow-capped peaks appearing dwarfed by their own immense pedestal. Precisely because of its influence on the local ecology and land use, the Gikuyu consider it to be an intimate part of Ngai's creation. It is a source of many rivers and streams that feed most of the Gikuyu country. The people associate Mount Kenya with strength, height, beauty and as a source of water, rain, and forest that the Gikuyu need for their survival. (p. 93)

There is a nexus between divine status of the Mountain and its ecological impact on the fertility and hence economic productivity to the Agikuyu community. The snow cap elevates its beauty and the presence of rivers enhance the fertility of the land for the sustenance of the community. The productive land that supports farming and the wellbeing of the community stands out as god in itself. This is what Karangi means when he says the land is an "intimate part of Ngai". Mother Nature in this community stands out as god to be worshipped as it provides the economic sustenance for the Agikuyu. That is why Ngugi complains about land degradation under the colonial regime in *A Grain of Wheat* as it is spiritually significant to the Agikuyu people. He writes, "[t]here were no crops on the land and what with the dried up weeds, gararaku, micege, mikengeria—and the sun, the country appeared sick and dull" (p. 14). The description suggests the advent of drought, which in Agikuyu cosmology is Ngai's curse owing to the desecration of land (Ngai) by foreigners.

Another essential aspect of the Agikuyu religion is the role of trees in the lives of humanity. According to Karangi, "Gikuyu, the founding father of the Agikuyu was given the land full of trees, water and ravines" (p. 114). In Ngugi's *River Between*, Chege tells his son the medicinal values of trees as they trudge towards the sacred groove. He says:

> But when Chege stopped near a certain tree or bush,
> Waiyaki knew that his father had something to explain.
> "The bark of that tree is good for a fresh wound."
> "The roots of this plant are good. When your stomach bites you, you boil them in water.
> Drink the liquid."
> And sometimes it would be a warning against that tree, "whose fruit is full of poison."
> Waiyaki felt close to his father as he had never felt before.

(p. 10)

The trees arising from Mother Nature contribute to the physical wellness of the people; the barks treat fresh wounds and roots treat stomach problems. The fruit of the land is therefore instrumental in the resuscitation of life. Waiyaki is therefore very happy because he is being introduced into great secrets of the divine through ecological education, which is tantamount to spiritual education. Chebii, Muthee and Kiemo (2020), observe that the colonial government outlawed herbal medicine through witchcraft act of

1925 (Para, 6). This is possibly because of the spiritual nature of herbal medicine.

The forest was also essential for hosting rites that facilitate the perpetuation of the community. In *A Grain of Wheat* the forest host dances among the young people who have designs on each other. Gikonyo, Karanja and Kihika meet young women such as Mumbi and Wambuku in the forests and socialize with each other. The narrator says:

> Kihika and Wambuku found an open place in the sun. The thick part of the forest, the dancers in the wood, and the hungry eyes of Njeri were behind them. Here green wattle trees and bush sloped steeply into the valley below. The valley sprawled flat for a distance and then bounced into the ridge of small hills. Beyond, and to the right, Kihika could just trace the outlines of Mahee Police Station, a symbol of that might which dominated Kenya to the door of every hut. (p. 39).

The forest cover provides the young people with an opportunity to date, chat and share political news affecting the people. The topography of the land offers the privacy required for the young people to bond. Wambuku has designs on Kihika as Gikonyo and Karanja compete over Mumbi. They play the guitar to woo her, and Karanja seems to be better musician than Gikonyo. Similarly, initiates in The River Between are taken to the forest to be treated and counselled to become men. The narrator says, "[t]he hospital was a small shed a little distance from the village. The floor was hard with bumps. A thin covering of grass and banana leaves was their bed. After two days Waiyaki's wound had swollen so much that he began to doubt if he would ever be well again. Perhaps he would lose his manhood" (p.30). They are exposed to hardship as a training to bear with the challenges of adult life. Later when Waiyaki falls in love with Nyambura, they meet is a bushy neighboiurhood, which Ngugi describes as "... bush, extending until it merged with the low-lying forest. The forest went down the slope to the Honia river. Beyond and across the valley facing Kameno was Makuyu, with many huts lying along the top in little clusters" (p. 50)

REFERENCES

Artwood M. (2015). The Maori People and Environmental Protectionism. Berkely Center for Religion, Peace and World Affairs. https://berkleycenter.georgetown.edu/posts/the-maori-people-and-environmental-protectionism.

Adoyoye, A. E. (2020). Mother Earth, Mother Africa: African indigenous religions. Garamond: African Sun Media.

Canfield M. (2011). Renewing Maoritanga: Ecological healing for a postcolonial world in Keri Hulme's *The bone people*, Witi ihimaera's *The Whale Rider*, and Patricia

Grace's Potiki. MA Thesis: East Carolina University. https://core.ac.uk/download/pdf/71973528.pdf.

Chebii, W.K., Muthee, J.K. & Kiemo, K. (2020).The governance of traditional medicine and

Herbal remedies in the selected local markets of Western Kenya. *J Ethnobiology Ethnomedicine* **16,** 39 (2020). https://doi.org/10.1186/s13002-020-00389-x.

Farah, N. (1998). *Secrets.* New York: Arcade Publishing, Inc.

Karang, M. M. (2005). The Sacred Mugumo Tree: Revisiting the Rots of Gikuyu Cosmology and Worship: A case Study of Gicugu Gikuyu of Kirinyaga District in Kenya. PhD Thesis, University of London.

Mire, S. (2015). *Wagar*, Fertility and Phallic Stelae: Cushitic Sky-God Belief and the Site of

Saint Aw-Barkhadle, Somaliland. *Afr Archaeol Rev* **32,** 93–109 (2015). https://doi.org/10.1007/s10437-015-9181-z.

Okasha, A. and Okasha, T. (2012). Religion, Spirituality and the Concept of Mental Illness. *Actasesp Psiquaia* 40 (2): pp 73-79.

Richards L. (2020). The Ancient Egyptian Conception of God: From the Predynastic Through the Old Kingdom(ca. 3800–2135 B.C.E.). *Journal of Semitics.* 29. 2. DOI: 10.25159/2663-6573/7244.

CHAPTER FIVE

Ecology and Pathology: Mother Nature and Mental Illness in Contemporary Postcolonial Literatures

> colonialism is a systematised negation of the other, a frenzied attempt to deny the other any attribute of humanity...which if left unchallenged by armed resistance, the colonized's defenses collapse and many of them end up in psychiatric institutions.
>
> Fanon,1961 p. 182

Postcolonial literary writers tend to associate mental illness with homocentric causes for example strands of othering such as political, economic and cultural othering of minority groups. Fanon in the above quote is one of these writers that suggest that mental illness arises from colonialism, which is tantamount to racial and political othering of the Africans in Algeria. As a result of the political oppression, the psyches of the Algerian soldiers collapse and "symptoms of madness become a sequel of the oppression" (182). Alternative voice however associate mental illness with ecological conditions in which human persons live. Rusell et al. observe that "nature or ecosystem contributes to human well-being. Nature affects the physical, mental, spiritual health, inspiration and identity" (p. 473) of human beings. Rusell et al. therefore challenge the homocentric problemitisation of mental illness and underscore the pertinent influence of Mother Nature in its genesis and development. Susan Williams (2017) writes:

> More subtle and indirect effects of climate change can add stress to people's lives in varying degrees. Whether experienced indirectly or directly, stressors to our climate translate into impaired mental health that can result in depression and anxiety. Although everyone is able to cope with a certain amount of stress, the accumulated effects of compound stress can tip a person from mentally healthy to mentally ill. (p.14)

Williams suggests that climate change affects mental health of people directly or indirectly by causing depression and anxiety that gradually develops into mental illness. This line of thought rejects Fanon's that limits mental illness to human attributes at the expense of ecological concerns that have long lasting effects society at large. Anxiety and self-alienation are not just caused by human related cause, but issues related to Mother Nature. According to George Hegel (1967), self-alienation as a separation between the essence and its condition. Hegel adds that it is through culture that the individual gives form to itself. As much as most scholars delimit Hegel's "condition" to social factors, this study extends it to the ecological condition. The term "culture" also extends to ecological setting of the self, and so characters that detest their ecological condition also suffer from self-alienation, which is psychologically disabling. While social conditions such as racial othering can be mitigated by political solutions, ecological factors require more than political will to eradicate.

This chapter therefore takes eco-centric perspective in the study of madness and the fragmented self in contemporary works of prose fiction. The texts to be studied in the chapter are Nyongesa's *The Endless Battle*, Rhys *Voyage in the Dark* and El Saadawi's *God Dies by the Nile*.

5.1 Hot, Dry Weather and Mental Illness: The Fragmented Self and Disorders of the Self

Cold temperatures lead to decreases in the incidence of negative mental health outcomes and hot temperatures lead to [their] increases

Mullins and White (2019, p. 2)

Mental illness in Nyongesa's *The Endless Battle* takes Mullins and Whites trajectory because characters are so affected by high temperatures that they exhibit symptoms of the fragmented self and disorders of the self. In the novel, the protagonist, Eugene migrates from Nairobi to Mandera, a semi-arid part of Kenya. Right from the journey, Eugene notices that the passengers, mostly Somalis, behave differently from the Kenyans he has met in Nairobi. As soon as he boards the bus in Nairobi, Eugene observes, "[t]he passengers most of who were manderans, jammed every nook of the bus […]. They were an impatient and irritable people: 'move you fool!' an elderly man barked" (p. 57). The people Eugene has lived with in Nairobi are not as irritable as the people of Mandera on the bus. Eugene is surprised to witness expletives being cast by adults to each other. For example, when a girl accidentally pushes an elderly woman, she snarls, "sharmute! Sharmute!" which is a Somali word for prostitute (p.57). Budhadeb Gosh (2020) refers to this type of behaviour as mood disorder, which is symptom of mental illness. The patients shift from calmness to excessive hostility without a justifiable reason. This is the same behaviour that Zakeya in El Saadawi's *God Dies by the Nile* exhibits. As much as focus on Zakeya's madness has been associated with patriarchal and class oppression, the writer begins her story by underscoring the hot sun:

> The sun rose up in the sky gradually. Its disc turned into a ball of fire, choking the wind, bearing down on the trees, turning everything into solid dryness, so that all things seemed to suffocate, burn in its red fire, and dry up, except the rivulets of sweat pouring down from Zakeya's face and body onto the ground. Beneath the sweat her face was livid like the face of the buffalo turning round and round beneath its yoke. (p.17)....

In this excerpt, Saadawi suggests that the hot ecological conditions result in Zakeya's lividness, which to a great extent triggers her mental illness. The temperatures are so high that everything seems to suffocate. According to Buell, writers with a concern for ecological environment will make deliberate references to Mother Nature to demonstrate environmental degradation (9). These harsh climatic conditions have adversely affected the economic conditions of Zakeya's family, which partly contribute to her fragmented self. She is engrossed in flashbacks that demonstrate its traumatized condition because of the poverty she was brought up in. She remembers her father's indigent state, "[a]ll that remained of him in her memory was a pair of long, thin, spindly legs, with protruding knees, a *galabeya* with its tail lifted and tied around his waist, a huge hoe held tightly in his big hands, as it rose and fell with a regular thud" (p.19). Zakeya's father is terribly thin, with knees protruding because he earns nothing from decades of peasantry on his farm. Mother Nature has constantly diminished the agricultural productivity of his land. The image of his emaciated being traumatizes his daughter Zakeya and it is absurd to blame her mental illness solely on homocentric reasons such as gender othering. Christopher Ball and Jennifer Little (2006) assert that flashbacks like Zakeya's confirm how the character's life has been disrupted (175). The disruption is a reference to pathological conditions to suggest that flashbacks in one's life are symptoms of mental illness

Similarly, characters in Nyongesa's *The Endless Battle* have emotional problems because of a hostile ecological environment. Indeed most of the anger tantrums on the bus are associated with change in temperature as a result of the ecological conditions. The narrator says:

> The ventilation became very poor and babies began to wail. The wails mingled with blowing of noses and throwing of phlegm to create shocking mnemonic of violence. The irate elderly man, next to Eugene, pulled his phlegm, leant over Eugene to open the window pane and spat. The detestable spittle came face to face with the draught and scattered on Eugene and other passengers. 'Ugh" don't do that!' admonished Eugene. 'Athon! Athon!' the passenger growled at him. (p. 58).

There is hostility exhibited towards Eugene by the Somali passengers, but arising from the ecological conditions such as high temperatures. The ventilation becomes poor and heightens the temperature in the bus; while the children "wail" the elders through phlegm and defend culprits against those who complain. The elderly man is referred to as "irate" to demonstrate his irritability as a result of the exposure to high temperatures. The phrase "mnemonics of violence" is reference to excessive hostility that Ghosh identifies as one of the major symptoms of mental illness. In the ensuing conversation, the passengers use more derogatory terms when Eugene tries to challenge their views. Eugene is shocked to hear expletives such as "Ngurale", a Somali term for "black man with tufty hair" –a snide reference to bantus– and "kaffir" a man without religion.

The narrator singles out heat stress and poverty as the major causes of this irritability. The ecological conditions of the areas that the bus is passing through because of poverty and the heat stress. The poverty is evident when the bus creates its own routes because of poor road network. The bus "hit potholes, swung passengers up and accelerated. Babies cried, girls wept and men complained" (p. 64). The weeping of girls and complaining of men signifies irritability and other mood disorders, which are symptoms of mental illness. The narrator concludes that the weeping and complaining (mental illness) is a "lamentation against inhumanity of nature" (p. 64). At this point, the narrator suggests that when Mother Nature is neglected, she retaliates against humankind by providing unfavourable conditions that cause mental illness. The narrator outlines these conditions, "[t]he vegetation dwindled into scrubs that covered thousands of acres. Sand, likewise possessed the largest part of the region" (p. 64). The lack of vegetation compounds the ecological hostility toward humankind as the bus approaches the semi-arid Garissa town. Eugene says:

> There is no one as vengeful as Nature [...] although she was patient with human weaknesses, once provoked, her vengeance was unbearable. She sauted human bodies, fetched whirlwinds from distant places that gathered tonnes of dust to spray them on people. The dust slapped windows and pierced their eyes. The sun breached down at its fiercest and weariness overwhelmed them. The heat stress nurtured an impatience and despair in you and unless you were careful you would be easily be overtaken by tantrums. (P. 64)

In this passage, Mother Nature's wrath or revenge is depicted through a number of consequences on humankind. As Buell suggests in his assertion that environment is a process, this excerpt implies that as a result of environmental neglect, Nature retaliates against humankind through violent whirlwinds that bring about dust storms, the hot sun that make our lives uncomfortable and, finally, the heat stress that destabilizes our mental health. The "impatience", "despair" and "tantrums" are among those aspects that Gosh singles out as mood disorders hence mental illness.

The harsh climatic conditions and mental ill-health dehumanizes characters and most of them exhibit shocking indifference and callousness. They associate living values such as mercy, love, humility and kindness with weakness. Eugene is surprised when Dinow, one of the passengers, laughs at the poor nomad who appears in the sparsely populated Modica. While Eugene sympathizes with the so called Mr "Faceless", Dinow asserts that they do not cry in this desert; "when angry, we just slaughter" (p. 66). Eugene condemns that as inhuman, but Dinow blames Mother Nature, "[s]ee the hot sun, man! You can't be soft here.it has vaporized our feelings" (p. 66). Dinow's reference to callousness reiterates Ronald Laing (1960)' concept of the unembodied self. For Laing, trauma causes a split between the mind and the body and the self's main functions become "observation, control and criticism" (p. 69). Laing refers to these patients as schizoids because the hollowness in heart destroys their relationships with fellow human beings and focus on relationship with self. Dinow and other characters from Mandera, on the bus exhibit schizoid symptoms such as excessive control, criticism and general inhumanity.

Other psychologists such as Kohut and Wolf refer to such a condition as the *unburdened self*. Because the persons were neglected in early life, they experience the surroundings as hostile. The victims therefore dream of living in a poisoned atmosphere or surrounded by swarms of hornets, they complain of noise and unpleasant odours and maintain a general attitude of irritability and suspiciousness (419). As much Kohut and Wolf delimit the characters negligence to homocentric aspects such as family, Mother Nature plays an essential role in neglecting her victims. The Mayor in Saadawi's *God Dies by the Nile* is one such a character, whose constant irritability and callousness arise from Mother Nature's hostility. In his conversations with subordinates such as Haj Ismail, they just have to be careful not to offend him. When Ismail comments about the inability of the poor to distinguish tastes of different things, the Mayor keeps quiet and Ismail is very worried because he does not know what to do to please him. In an obsequious tone, Haj Ismail says, "[y]our highness, what I meant is that everything tastes bitter to the mouth of a peasant' (p.27). Unable to overcome the jealousy he has for his brother, the Mayor turns his anger towards innocent people such as Kaffrawi. He just stands up and tells Hajj Ismail, "[b]oy, bring the handcuffs and chains immediately," (p. 28), to arrest Kaffrawi. This is the irritability typical of the *unburdened self* he has acquired from the hostile ecological environment.

This is a similar experience in Nyongesa's *The Endless Battle* albeit among people of the lower classes. The unburdened self therefore affects both the dominant group and marginalized groups. For example, when Eugene boards the bus and complains against elders careless spitting, he comes under heavy criticism. The elder blurts, "[u]seless man, dog!" Another elder says,'[i]f he wants comfort, let him buy his car" (p. 59). Before Eugene can think about that another man quotes a proverb, "[o]ur people say a journey has no pleasure", only to be corrected by a youth, "don't waste such wisdom on *ngurale*. These dogs have no brains. They only think of what lies inside our girls' dresses" (p.59). Besides having symptoms of the *unburdened self*, all this criticism among these characters confirms Laing's concept of the schizoid. These characters are schizoids as illustrated by the inhumanity of their expletives as they seek to control Eugene. The proverb "journey has no pleasure" is demonstrates desire to alienate oneself from the reality of poor roads to get solace. For Laing, the schizoid abandons reality and conceals behind abstraction for example wisdom, religion or hallucinations. The hostile ecological setting has diminished "the body" such that characters have to be "disembodied" to face life's realities. According to Laing, the body refers normal human beings with a sense of personal continuity, with bodily desire to gratify and natural fear that physical injury can harm their flesh and blood (67). But tendency to cast aspersions at normal bodily functions such as sex, eating, celebrations and other is a symptom of the unembodied self. The young man's description of Bantus (Ngurale) as "dogs" because they think about sex enlists him among schizoids. He is unembodied and according to Rudolph Bultmann (1972) such patients have an eccentric desire to disentangle oneself from the body and achieve a mystic state of spirituality (p. 169). Indeed, most of the characters converse about their religion on the bus and believe everything that happens, however irrational has been predetermined by the deity. Dinow tells Eugene that even his journey to Mandera was predetermined by the deity (p. 66) and so they have no control over it. This assertion exhibits the schizoid surrender of all responsibility because of the terrible experiences they have had. According to Laing, the unembodied self is "frightened of the world, afraid that any impingement will be implosive, penetrative, fragmenting and engulfing; he is afraid of coming out of himself" (83). The experiences they have had in their ecological settings such as droughts, death of livestock, raids by enemy clans and famine subject them to fear of any desire to control their destiny. The religious fanaticism shows human surrender to the hostile ecological conditions that have the pre-eminence in their motherland.

The constant references to religion and objectification of sex is also evident when Eugene brings his wife, Fresher to his school without informing the principal the facts of their relationship. The principal says, "[y]ou are cohabiting and Muslims hate it" (p. 76). The religious references are aimed at shifting the characters to what Bailey (1942) denotes as "consciousness so strongly oriented in directions other than those of physical existence" (p. 4), which are symptoms of dissociation. Being schizoids by nature, the Somali characters in the novel gradually influence Eugene towards the condition through constant attacks on his embodied state.

One devastating attack that facilitates his shift to depression and unembodied self is the landlady's derogatory comments on their sex life. Having been sacked at Zeitun High school, Fresher is again accused of making loud groans during love making. The land lady says they must move from their rental house because she is a "prostitute ....make noise during love making at night" (p. 81). She even advises Eugene to marry a circumcised girl to eradicate the noise making. These comments result in Eugene's depression, which according to Richard Gray (p. 264) is a symptom of a pathological condition referred to as the fragmented self. He writes of the fragmented self "[t]he victim suffers from self-doubt, in severe depression; a fractured person seeking for some regular pattern in the little, broken life." Eugene's life exhibits these aspects of pathology as he starts finding it difficult to make love with his wife.

Eugene at this point is more interested in what Laing refers to as imagos rather than his wife. Whereas the religious schizoids turn to hallucinations, Eugene's and Mayor's focus turn to pornography and sexual perversions. The Mayor in *God Dies by the Nile* displaces all his incapacitation to sexual perversions, for example when comparing himself with his brother, he goes into hallucination to meditate the nightclubs of Cairo "[t]he women dancing, their bodies moving, their perfume and soft laughter going through him" (p. 23). These sexual images are also evident when he uses Muslim clerics to trick Zeinab into his house; he thinks, "Her full lips were a natural red, and slightly moist like a flower in the morning dew. Her breasts were round, firm, upturned with the sharp outlines of healthy flesh" (p. 104). The Mayor, like other schizoids, seems to derive sexual pleasure from sexual images.

Similarly, Eugene is obsessed with sexual images and perversions when his wife returns to their Nairobi home. The ecological environment and cultural conditions it has created in Mandera maintain their control over Eugene's life. This stands out through bolstering religious beliefs and circumcision of women, which Eugene and Fresher do not uphold because they hail from a place with different ecological conditions. Without a religion and wife to turn to, Eugene becomes a pornography addict, which is an element of the fragmented self. According to Laing, the schizoid's self turns from realities to imagos (p. 74), and this is Eugene's condition. He loses interest in his wife and gets stuck to images to reduce the anxiety he faces. The narrator says of Eugene:

> His manners had changed. He wanted to be alone most times, his gaze firmly fixed on the phone. It surprised Fresher which scrumptious subjects glued her husband on the phone. He responded nervously whenever she drew closer and seemed to avoid eye contact. When she made any negative remark, he could growl and scowl at her. Her husband had become very aggressive. He had complained of constant bouts of insomnia for the previous two months. His looks had a lot to desire. His cheekbone protruded and eyes were sunken. The dressing was no exception: he dressed shabbily, so unlike the noble Eugene he had married nine years earlier. (P. 85)

This passage confirms how five years in Mandera, a hot region in Kenya, have changed Eugene's mental health. First, he is a pornography addict to demonstrate how his self has shifted to the unembodied state that only appreciates abstractions. Secondly, he is always nervous when his wife comes closer to him; this anxiety stems from the new ecological environment that chastised his sexual life. His principal's decision to accuse him of cohabiting (contravenes Islam) and landlady's eviction because his wife is uncircumcised, sow the fear for sex and wife. According to Johson (1963), the withdrawal of the psychologically alienated person is meant to "reduce external contact to minimize conflict and hence anxiety" (p. 371). Eugene is therefore psychologically alienated to minimize the conflict with his Mandera neighbours. Given that the ecological environment has bolstered religious fanaticism, he cannot socialize with women and girls in his environment and resorts to imagos and hand practice. Eugene's looks underscore his pathological condition. Gerald Davison et.al refer to Eugene's condition as avolition; a patient loses interest in routine activities. They neglect their personal hygiene and move around with uncombed hair, dirty nails, unbrushed teeth and tattered clothes. They have challenges in doing their work, household chores and spend most of their time sitting around doing nothing (p. 329). Eugene just idles in the house over the holidays, shabbily dressed surfing the internet for pornography. When Fresher goes through the Google history of his phone, she comes across "naked pictures of women: plump , white with legs spread [...] PRETTY PORN LADIES, BEAUTIFUL NAKED WOMEN, SEXY NAKED GIRLS, MOST SEXY NAKED LADIES IN THE WORLD. She could now tell why her husband's gaze was on his phone" (p. 87). Eugene's self has turned to abstract pictures or what Laing refers to as imagos and therefore become unembodied as demonstrated by his erectile dysfunction. Fresher asks him a question that reveals his addiction to masturbation, "[i]f you watch this alone, you will desire to have sex, how do you relieve yourself?" (p. 87). Eugene becomes infuriated, but all evidence points towards his addiction to self sex: the anger tantrums, stammering and low libido.

The narrator says that "Eugene could do nothing. Nothing…he just touched and touched himself" (p. 83). The "touching" refers to self-stimulation for masturbation, which according to Kohut and Wolf (1978) the pathological condition is referred to as the *understimulated self,* a self-devoid of vitality, boring, apathetic and is experienced by others the same way (p. 418). Desperate for happiness, victims of the *understimulated self-*such as Eugene "stimulate themselves by addictive and promiscuous activities, perversions, gambling, drug and alcohol induced excitement and lifestyle characterized by hyper sociability" (p. 478). The hostile ecological conditions of Mandera compel Eugene to turn to "addictive" behaviours such as pornography and hand practice given that his wife leaves him and he cannot interact with the circumcised, Muslim girls in the region. This is the same character that is portrayed by Sheikh Metwali in *God Dies by the Nile.* Like the Mayor, Metwali is sexually perverted because he roams at night to exhume corpses to screw. He would exhume corpses "[a]nd if it was that of a female, he would crawl over it until his face was near the chin. If it was male, he turned it over on its face then crawled over it until the lower part of its belly pressed down on the buttocks from behind (p. 74). These acts of perversion are features of the *understimulated self* that affects people who are apathetic and feel very bored by ecological conditions.

Zakeya's pathological condition also arises from practices that stem from the ecological conditions of her region. Her late husband Abdel Moneim was brutal and as observed previously about attributes of the unburdened self, the hot and dry weather has made him callous and irritable. The narrator says that "[e]very time a son of hers died, he would strike out at her blindly" (p. 89). Moneim's brutality reiterates chapter three of this book in which the ecological environment leads to patriarchal tendencies. The patriarchal oppression leads to her current pathological condition with vivid dreams in which "she finds herself at the iron gate. Then she is lying on her mat with her husband Abdel Moneim and her son on the other. The husband hits her pregnant belly and proceeds to have sex with her (p. 88). All her trips to Al Sayeda do not bear any fruit; the clerics claim that she is possessed by an evil spirit.

Although homocentric perspectives will focus on culture such as patriarchy and gender othering as the prime causes of Eugene's, the Mayor's, Metwali's and Zakeya's pathological conditions, the ecological conditions of their regions bolster cultural practices such as religious fanaticism, female circumcision and patriarchy that objectify the characters. The hostile ecological environment for instance has overwhelmed the people such that they believe everything is predetermined. This belief in fate demonstrates the pre-eminence of Mother Nature over the characters in *Endless Battle* and *God Dies by the Nile*.

5.2 Cold Weather and Mental ill-health: The Fragmented Self in *Rhy's Voyage in the Dark*

Significant cold effects were also observed for depressive disorders and affective disorders in Shenzhen and Huizhou, the largest cumulative risks being 1.26.

(Zhang S., Yang Y., Xie X., et. al., 2020, p. 4)

As much as studies have associated the hot temperatures with mental health issues, emerging studies challenge it and single out cold temperatures as having an impact on certain pathological conditions. Shiyu Zhang et al. (2020) in their study in different regions in China observe that cold temperatures lead to depressive and affective disorders. These according to gray (2012) are aspects of the fragmented self and are prevalent in most Caribbean works of prose fiction. In Velma Pollards' *Homestretch* for instance, characters such as Brenda complain a great deal about the cold temperatures in England.

This subchapter will examine the psychological effect of cold temperatures on characters in Rhys *Voyage in the Dark*. The heroine, Anna migrates from Caribbean to England, but life turns out to be extremely challenging to the point of affecting her mental health. Andres Cordera (2012) associates Ann's mental health challenges to the modernist homocentric perspective. He writes:

Anna's self is constructed as a blackened sexualized female and this helps to distinguish her subaltern position based on several colonial binaries such as master/slave, white/black and male/female. Post-colonial criticism claims that those binaries entail a violent hierarchy in which one opposite is always dominant over the other. (p. 4).

According to Cordera, the racial and political othering of the people of colour in Caribbean is behind Ann's psychological fragmentation. They occupy the subaltern position and so the dominant group discriminates them such that their psyche is affected. While Cordera takes Fanon's trajectory in the analysis of the mental condition of the marginalized groups, this subchapter takes an ecological perspective that links Anna's pathological condition to the ecological conditions of the host nation, England.

From the first day of her arrival in England, Anna singles out the ecological conditions of England as the cause of her depression. Anna says:

> Lying between 15.10 and 15.40 degrees N and 61.14 and 61.30 degrees W. 'A goodly island and something highland, but all overgrown with woods,' that book said. And all crumpled into hills and mountains as you would crumple a piece of paper in your hand-rounded green hills and sharply-cut mountains. A curtain fell and I was here. This England Hester said and I watched it through the train window divided into squares like pocket-hand-kerchiefs. (p. 15)

Ann has insurmountable disdain for England and demonstrated by the sarcasm in the first sentences of this extract. That in spite of England's goodness, it is surrounded with "overgrown …woods" that cause its severe coldness particularly in winter. The contemptuous attitude is evident when the hills are compared to "crumpled" or folded pieces of paper. Her coming to England is described as an unfortunate incident in her life because "the curtain" falls to compel he migration. The physical planning of the host nation is detestable to Ann; she compares the physical planning to squares on a pocket handkerchief" to confirm her disdainful attitude towards the nation. Ann dislikes even the houses because of the cold winter season; she describe them as "dark houses all alike frowning one after the other" (p. 16), and from the outset concludes, "I am not going to like this place, I am not going to like this place" (p.16). Ann's assertions at this beginning of the novel are inconsistent to Cordera's homocentric perspective that associates her depression with racial and political othering. The downpour intensifies her depression. She says, "[w]hen we were coming home from the theatre that night, it began to rain and in Brighton, it rained all the time. We got to Holloway and it was winter and the dark streets round the theatre made me think of the murders" (p. 16). Ann is gradually traumatized by the ecological environment in which she lives. According to Vito Zepenic (2016), trauma causes self-disintegration in three directions: First is suffocation of capabilities of the self in which the self is incapable of adapting thereby losing the requisite competence for success in life (84). Ann cannot function very well in her relationships because of the pain in her heart. Whether her friends throw some jibes at her or want to show her love, Anna starts crying. For example, Dr

Ames' remarks on people's jibes on her being virgin provoke her to tears. She says, "[b]ut I felt cold, as if someone had thrown cold water over me. When he kissed me I began to cry" (p. 32). Ann's belief that England is cold affects herself such that she cannot sustain a romantic relationship with men. She associated all the men in England with the coldness typical of the ecological conditions. When Joe tries to show her his love, she says, "[n]o, don't [...]do leave me alone, do leave me alone" (p. 109). Then she began to cry; Joe is touched by this and after assessing the situation, he discovers that Anna is being affected by the cold ecological environment. He says, "[d]on't cry [...] I'll better go and get something to put over you. This room is as cold as hell" (p. 109). As Zhang et. al assert in the introduction, Joe suggests that Ann's depression arises from the cold winter.

Secondly, Zepenic asserts that trauma results in losing of interest in others as the person loses relationships: they are ignored, rejected, unliked, unloved, feels worthless and insecure. Throughout Anna's life in England, she does not mention any close friends with whom she has lasting relationships. When male friends who pay her visits, her landlady detests it just because of her sickly condition and propensity to have so many male partners. Ann cannot maintain one relationship and be wooed for marriage. In her sickly state, the landlady bawls at her:

> I don't hold with the way you go on, if you want to know, and my husband don't neither. Crawling up the stairs at 3 o'clock in the morning. And then today dressed up to the nines. I've got eyes in my head [...] I won't have you calling

me a liar [...]you and your drawly voice. And if you give me any of your lip, I'll have my husband up to you. (P. 26)

The crux of the landlady's message is that Ann should be able to maintain one male partner and possibly marry him to stay in the room. Her odd personality has denied her this and therefore welcomes many partners that adversely affects the reputation of the house. The mention of Ann's "drawly voice" refers to her depressed state that the ecological environment has exposed her and ruined her chances of establishing a stable relationships. As Zepenic suggests, the landlady in this excerpt rejects her and she feels "unloved and insecure." Before the row, Ann realizes that the landlady has not laid the fire that Ann had requested, and when she requests her to provide tea to warm herself, the landlady blurts, "[y]ou seem to think I am here to wait on you," (p. 26). Besides the landlady's rejection, some men also reject her because of her depressed condition. Ann chooses black clothes, which reflect the dark state of herself and Mr Jeffries does not like it. He asks, "[d]o you always wear black?" (p. 17), and he gives his negative judgement, "[y]ou looked awfully pathetic when you were choosing those horrible stockings so anxiously" (p. 20). These assertions demonstrate Ann's rejection by those around her.

The third effect of trauma according to Zepenic is disintegration of the self or sense of fragmentation, which manifests through inner disharmony, conflict, doubt, sense of loss, discontinuation and disunion of the self (87), all of which are Anna's experiences in *Voyage in the Dark*. An exhibit of internal conflicts in many instances as a result of the trauma from her ecological environment, Ann's story is characterised by images of "coldness" and "sickness" that mirror the English ecological environment. It is a winter season throughout *Voyage in the Dark* and when Ann meets Joe, she tells him, "I feel awfully sick" (p. 106). The sickness suggests the fragmented self that Zepenic refers as inner disharmony while Richard Gray et al. refers to as "fractured self, seeking for the elusive wholeness" (124). Ann's suggests that the sickness first stems from the ecological environment because she "felt cold" and "pulled the eiderdown" over her shoulders and slept in her bed (p. 106). Her friend Joe was sitting near the fire, laughing with his acquaintances.

As soon as Joe mentions that Laurie was born in Caribbean and he knew her father Morgan, Ann explodes and casts expletives at him.

> You are a liar […] you didn't know my father because my real name isn't Morgan and I will never tell you my real name and I was born in Manchester and I will never tell you anything real about myself. Everything I tell you about myself is a lie [...] oh go to hell and get off this bed. You get on my nerves. (P. 107)

This episode demonstrates Ann's fragmentation that manifests through inner conflict; although she is "Ann Morgan" she publicly denies this identity. The truth is that she was born in Caribbean, but she denies it and says she was born in Manchester, England. The sentence "I will never tell you anything real about myself" confirms Laing's assertion that the unembodied self is "frightened of the world, afraid that any impingement will be implosive, penetrative, fragmenting and engulfing; he[sic] is afraid of coming out of himself [sic]" (83). The violence is an expression of this fear that constitutes the largest proportion of her sickness. Her violence compels Laurie and Joe to direct her to another room after her demand. But when she reaches there, she does dislikes the room again. She says, "[t]here was no fire. There was no key in the lock [...]it was as cold as being in the street" (p.108). It is irrational how she left a warmer room over to go to a room without fire for starting unnecessary commotion with Laurie. All she wanted was to end her relationship with Joe and Laurie because she associates them with the cold and wintry, England. Joe follows her to the room and when he comments that Laurie is "a tart", Ann defends Laurie against the accusation, "[w]hy shouldn't she be a tart? It is just as good as anything else, as far as I can see" (p.108). She then tells Joe, "do leave me alone, do leave me alone" and breaks down (p. 109). Her sudden change to defend Laurie refers to the ambivalence of in-between identities. According to Homi Bhabha (1994), in-between identities are characterized by "here" nor "there"; both "this and that" and neither this nor that" (227). In the above extract, Ann loves Caribbean and changes tune to love England. She dislikes Laurie, but when Joe criticizes her, she changes to like her. She hates the first room, but when she moves to the second one, she changes to appreciate the first. The crying that proceeds the ambivalence is the pathological condition that stems from constant shift of identities as a result of ambivalence. Ann's act of crying also signifies Zepenic's "discontinuation" as the patient desires to end all their relationships or connection to others.

Indeed Ann is unable to maintain love relationships, for example she fails to hold onto Walter in spite of his love for her. In one of his letters to her, he writes, "shy Anna, I love you so much, always, Walter" (p. 148). But as soon as he moves to Paris, she makes love with different men and ends up pregnant. Vincent confirms that Walter had a plan to settle down with her, but Anna's unsettled self ruins the relationship. Vincent says "[y]ou must have known that Walter would look after you. And he had fixed everything up" (p. 147). But now the news Vincent receives is she pregnant from a man she cannot tell, "[o]h I don't mean it is Walters. I don't know whose it is" (p. 146). Anna's inability to tell the father of her baby parallels her lack of permanent abode; hence her unstable self that denies her home and family. Betrayed, Vincent asks her to return all the letters Walter wrote to her, but promises to foot her abortion bill at Mrs Robison's flat.

Conclusion

This chapter set out to analyse the nexus between the ecological environment and mental illness in three works of prose fiction, Rhy's *Voyage in the Dark*, Nyongesa's *Endless Battle* and Saadawi's *God Dies by the Nile*. From the foregoing discussion, it is apparent that mental illness does not just arise from homocentric factors but ecological factors such as hot and dry weather or cold and wet weather affect characters mental health. Whereas hot and dry climates affect Eugene's and Zakeya's mental health in The Endless Battle and *God Dies by the Nile,* Anna's self is affected by the coldness of England.

REFERENCES

Ball, C. and Little J. (2006). "A Comparison of Involuntary Autobiographical Memory Retrievals." Applied Cognitive Psychology 20: 1167–1179.

Bultmann, R. (1972). *Primitive Christianity in its Contemporary Setting*. World Publishing.

Cordera, A. (2012). *Divided Self in Jean Rhys' Voyage in the Dark*. White Rabbit: *English Studies in Latin America 4*. Available from: https://www.researchgate.net/publication/353647153_Divided_Self_in_Jean_Rhys'_Voyage_in_the_Dark.

Davison, Gerald et al. *Abnormal Psychology*. Ontario: John Wiley & Sons, 2008

Ghosh, B. Gosh (2020). Mental Illness: Symptoms and Evaluation. https://www.researchgate.net/publication/344688054_Mental_Illness_Symptoms_and_Evaluation.

Gray, Richard, et al. *A Frantz Kafka Encyclopaedia*. London: Greenswood Press, 2005.

Hegel, G. (1967). *The Phenology of the Mind*, trans. J.B. Baille. Harper & Row Publishers.

Johnson, F. (1963). Psychological Alienation: Isolation and Self Estrangement. *Psychoanalytic Review*, 62. 3: P. 369- 405.

Laing D. R. (1960). *The Divided Self: An Existential Study of Sanity and Madness.* Penguin.

Mullins, J. T., & White, C. (2019). Temperature and mental health: Evidence from the spectrum of mental health outcomes. *Journal of Health Economics,* 102240. https://doi.org/10.1016/j.jhealeco.2019.102240.

Nyongesa A. (2016). *The Endless Battle.* Nairobi. Royallite Publishers.
Rhys. J. (1934). *Voyage in the Dark.* New York: Penguin Books.
Russell, R., Guerry, A. D., Balvanera, P., Gould, R. K., Basurto, X., Chan, K. M., ... & Tam, J. (2013). Humans and nature: how knowing and experiencing nature affect well-being. *Annual Review of Environment and Resources, 38,* 473–502. https://doi.org/10.1146/annurev-environ-012312-110838

Williams S. (2017). Mental Health and our Changing climate: Impacts, implications, and guidance. *American Psychological Association.* https://www.apa.org/news/press/releases/2017/03/mental-health-climate.pdf.

Zhang S., Yang Y., Xie. X., et al. The effect of temperature on cause-specific mental disorders in three subtropical cities: A case-crossover study in China. *Environment International,* 143. https://www.researchgate.net/publication/343020125 .

Zepenic, V. (2016). Disintegration of the Self Structure Caused Severe Trauma. *Psychology And Behaviour Sciences,* 5: 83-92.

6. CHAPTER SUMMARIES, CONCLUSIONS AND RECOMMENDATIONS FOR FUTURE STUDIES

In this study I set out to interrogate the influence of the ecological environment on desirable and undesirable cultural traditions in selected works of prose fiction, analyse the nexus between ecological environment and political systems in selected works of prose fiction, investigate the influence of ecological environment on religious aspects of characters in selected novels, analyse the nexus between ecological environment and slavery, colonialism and industrial revolution in selected works of prose fiction and finally, analyse the nexus between Mother Nature and mental health.

In the first chapter, I placed the study in context by expounding on the important voices related to the topic and how the study finds its gap. There is a cogent justification of the study and elaborate statement of the problem, which was stated as "[s]tudy transgresses the conventional tradition of highlighting ecological concerns in literary writing and instead shows how literary writers give Mother Nature her rightful place. Using eco-criticism, the study challenges homocentric attributes of literature and underscores the impact of the ecological environment in all human aspects of life. This analytical study is, therefore, a close textual reading of the primary and secondary texts while L. Buell (2005) serves as a theoretical framework for the interpretation." Besides Buell's tenets of eco-criticism, the ideas of other philosophers such as Bacon and Spendings were referred to give strong foundation to the study. For Bacon, the relationship between humanity and Mother Nature is symbiotic because for "Nature to be commanded must be obeyed". Bacon rejects superiority of humankind over Nature.

In Chapter Two, I demonstrated how the ecological environment compels communities to choose certain cultural practices in Farah's *From the Crooked Rib*, Kyalo Mativo's *On the Market Day*, Mohamed's *Black Mamba Boy* and John Steinbeck's *The Pearl*. In the chapter, it was clear that the ecological environment leads to cultural traditions such as infibulation in *From the Crooked Rib*, fishing, migrancy and violence in Mohamed's *Black Mamba Boy* Nyongesa's "Sordid Boon" and Steinbeck's *The Pearl*. Most of these practices were both desirable and undesirable to the contemporary society. The chapter had at least four essays on literary works from Africa and beyond

In Chapter Three I demonstrated how the influence of Mother Nature on slavery, colonialism and natural environment dictates the political structures of societies in selected works of prose fiction. Most communities living in arid or desert regions practice nomadic pastoralism and have had autocratic governments. Countries such as Somalia, Libya, Egypt, Algeria and Saudi Arabia have mostly been ruled by dictatorial regimes because of the prevailing ecological conditions that contribute to the choice of such systems of governments. Using ideas of scholars such as Kradin, it was discovered that democracy has not been a choice of leadership styles among nomads and this is possibly why it has always flopped in Egypt and Afghanistan. The so called democratic Mohamed Mursi's regime was overthrown by the Egyptian army in less than a year without complaints from the US, a bastion of democracy. After twenty-one years of American rule, democracy could not take root in Afghanistan and the Americans abandoned the weak democratic regime to be dethroned in less than six months by the autocratic Taliban. The ecological conditions therefore contributes to the system of government chosen people in a region. The study did not investigate the role of ecological factors on Laissez-faire system of leadership because of scarcity of literary works on the style.

In Chapter Four, I focused on the nexus between the ecological environment and religious aspects of characters in selected works of prose. The subchapters demonstrated how Mother Nature influences traditional religions in selected works of prose. The texts include Ngugi wa Thiong'os the *River Between,* Farah's *Secrets,* Mohamed's *Black Mamba Boy* and Witi Ihimera's *The Whale Rider.* It was interesting to observe that Mother Nature creates the first human being in the indigenous Maori religion as brought out in Ihimera's *The Whale Rider.* In Ngugi wa Thiong'o's *The River Between,* it was clear that the presence of Mount Kirinyaga determine the fundamental beliefs of Agikuyu religion and the presence of trees and birds form the foundation of the Somali pre-Islamic religion in Farah's Secrets and Mohamed's *Black Mamba Boy.* The study did not find any connection between Mother Nature and major world religions such as Islam, Christianity and Buddhism because scarcity of literary works on them. Some scholars content that among the Agikuyu, God is associated with femaleness because of the ability to provide and nurture the offspring. There was a parallel between this assertion and the expression "Mother Nature" instead of "Father Nature" that overturns homocentric perspectives that elevate patriarchy in the society.

In Chapter Five, I set out to analyse the nexus between the ecological environment and mental illness in three works of prose fiction, Rhy's *Voyage in the Dark*, Nyongesa's *Endless Battle* and Saadawi's *God Dies by the Nile*. From the discussion, it was apparent that mental illness does not just arise from homocentric factors such as othering and physiology, but ecological factors such as hot and dry weather or cold and wet weather. Whereas hot and dry climates affect Eugene's and Zakeya's mental health in *The Endless Battle* and *God Dies by the Nile*, Anna's self is affected by the coldness of England in Rhys' *Voyage in the Dark*. Several disorders of the self such as the *understimulated self* and *unburdened self* were identified in both rich and poor classes in characters living in hostile weather conditions.

Recommendations for Future Tasks:

Eco-criticism is a nascent critical approach that has pervaded both literary creation and criticism with the emergence of climate change. Writers have the burden to reflect the teething

Psychological and social problems that come with climate change. From the Bacon's philosophy at the advent of scientific revolution to the industrial revolution in the eightieth century, few scholars have thought about the place of Mother Nature in our world. Every field of study and worse still dominant religions tend to underscore the centrality of humanity in the ecosystem without an iota of thought about the ecosystem. The present study, on the centrality of Mother Nature was conducted under the stated scope and limitation of contemporary works of fiction. The following areas can form new directions for further scholarship in relation to present day study:

i) While study explored the impact of Mother Nature on character attributes, it did not investigate its influence on some attributes in fiction and poetry. Future studies should explore the influence of Mother Nature on certain characteristics such as human intelligence in contemporary works of fiction and poetry.

ii) The influence of Mother Nature on the fundamental beliefs of major religions of the world such as Islam, Christianity and Buddhism. This study investigated Mother Nature's impact on indigenous religions such as the Maori, Agikuyu and the Yoruba.

iii) The influence of Mother Nature on strains of pathology such as creative arts, schizophrenia and personality disorders should be extended. The study mostly dwelt on mild strains of pathology such as the fragmented self and disorders of the self. Why do certain nations have more singers and creative writers than others? Do ecological conditions contribute?

iv) The influence of ecological conditions on Laissez-faire system of leadership. While the studied found out the nexus between ecological conditions and autocracy and democracy, it did not explore the nexus between Nature and Laissez-faire.

v) The connection between divinity and femininity. It was interesting how the Agikuyu religion associated the God, Murungu with femininity. Future studies should extend this to major religions of the world, for example Christianity, Islam and Buddhism

Mmap Nonfiction and Academic books

If you have enjoyed **Re-centring Mother Earth: Ecological Reading of Contemporary Works of Fiction** consider these other fine *Nonfiction and Academic* books from Mwanaka Media and Publishing:

Cultural Hybridity and Fixity by Andrew Nyongesa
Tintinnabulation of Literary Theory by Andrew Nyongesa
South Africa and United Nations Peacekeeping Offensive Operations by Antonio Garcia
A Case of Love and Hate by Chenjerai Mhondera
A Cat and Mouse Affair by Bruno Shora
The Scholarship Girl by Abigail George
The Gods Sleep Through It All by Wonder Guchu
PHENOMENOLOGY OF DECOLONIZING THE UNIVERSITY: *Essays in the Contemporary Thoughts of Afrikology by Zvikomborero Kapuya*
Africanization and Americanization Anthology Volume 1, Searching for Interracial, Interstitial, Intersectional and Interstates Meeting Spaces, Africa Vs North America by Tendai R Mwanaka
Africa, UK and Ireland: Writing Politics and Knowledge Production Vol 1 by Tendai R Mwanaka
Writing Language, Culture and Development, Africa Vs Asia Vol 1 by Tendai R Mwanaka, Wanjohi wa Makokha and Upal Deb
Zimbolicious: An Anthology of Zimbabwean Literature and Arts, Vol 3 by Tendai Mwanaka
Drawing Without Licence by Tendai R Mwanaka
Writing Grandmothers/ Escribiendo sobre nuestras raíces: Africa Vs Latin America Vol 2 by Tendai R Mwanaka and Felix Rodriguez

Nationalism: (Mis)Understanding Donald Trump's Capitalism, Racism, Global Politics, International Trade and Media Wars, Africa Vs North America Vol 2 by Tendai R Mwanaka
It Is Not About Me: Diaries 2010-2011 by Tendai Rinos Mwanaka
Chitungwiza Mushamukuru: An Anthology from Zimbabwe's Biggest Ghetto Town by Tendai Rinos Mwanaka
The Day and the Dweller: A Study of the Emerald Tablets by Jonathan Thompson
Zimbolicious Anthology Vol 4: An Anthology of Zimbabwean Literature and Arts by Tendai Rinos Mwanaka and Jabulani Mzinyathi
Parks and Recreation by Abigail George
FAMILY LAW AND POLITICS WITH BIOLOGY AND ROYALTY IN AFRICA AND NORTH AMERICA by Peter Ateh-Afec Fossungo
Writing Robotics, Africa Vs Asia, Vol 2 by Tendai Rinos Mwanaka
Zimbolicious Anthology Vol 5: An Anthology of Zimbabwean Literature and Arts by Tendai R. Mwanaka
Love Notes: Everything is Love, An Anthology of Indigenous Languages of Africa and East Europe by Tendai R Mwanaka
Zimbolicious Anthology Vol 6: An Anthology of Zimbabwean Literature and Arts by Tendai R. Mwanaka and Chenjerai Mhondera
BATTLING LANGUAGE RIGHTS GOVERNANCE IN AFRICA: SWISSELGIANISM, UBACKISM, AND THE AMBAZONIA-CAMEROUN WAR by Peter Ateh-Afec Fossungo
Otherness and Pathology: The Fragmented Self and Madness in Contemporary African Fiction by Andrew Nyongesa

Upcoming
Zimbabwe: The Blame Game, New and Recollected essays and Non-fictions by Tendai Rinos Mwanaka
The Trick is to Keep Breathing: Covid 19 Stories From African and North American Writers, Vol 3 by Tendai Rinos Mwanaka
Zimbabwe: Beyond Robert Mugabe by Tendai Rinos Mwanaka

Zimbabwe: The Urgency Of Now, New and Recollected Essays and Non Fictions by Tendai Rinos Mwanaka

Language, Thought, Art and Existence: New and Recollected Essays and Non Fictions By Tendai Rinos Mwanaka

Fixing Earth Anthology: An anthology of Africa, UK and Ireland Writers, Vol 2 by Tendai Rinos Mwanaka

https://facebook.com/MwanakaMediaAndPublishing/

www.ingramcontent.com/pod-product-compliance
Lightning Source LLC
Chambersburg PA
CBHW011718220426
43663CB00020B/2927